W9-AAV-776

3 4028 03352 8333

WITHDRAWN

NW

There's A Branch
Near You

HARRIS COUNTY PUBLIC LIBRARY
HOUSTON, TEXAS

DEMCO

Put It Together, Put It Across

The Craft of Business Presentation

by
David Bernstein

With illustrations by Rex Audley

Cassell

Cassell Publishers Ltd.
Artillery House
Artillery Row
London SW1P 1RT

British Library Cataloguing in Publication Data

Bernstein, David
    Put it together, put it across: the
    craft of business presentation.
    1. Public speaking
    I. Title
    808.5'1   PN4121

    ISBN 0-304-31733-0

Typeset by Witwell Ltd, Southport
Printed and bound by Camelot Press
Copyright © 1988 by Cassell Publishers Ltd.

DEDICATION
To Peggy, Trevor and Prim

Contents

Preface

Most books I had read on business presentations seemed to concentrate on the art of delivery and the use of equipment. The craft – of structuring the argument, developing ideas – received far less attention.

I felt the need for a book which treated and related both skills – putting it together and putting it across.

In my researches I discovered a few Greeks and Romans who proved surprisingly relevant and very readable. More recently, of course, Antony Jay has mapped the territory. I am indebted to him and the other authors I quote. And even more to those I don't know I'm quoting.

In fact every speech I've heard, every presentation I've attended, has contributed to the text.

I want to thank all the organizations who invited me to speak, the audiences who participated and the production crews who endured my rehearsals. My especial thanks to clients and colleagues at The Creative Business, to Diane Hobson who began the task of transcribing my manuscript and Shirley Birtchnall who bore the brunt and suffered my moods with patience and wit.

My associates at the publishers, Simon Lake and Diana Russell, gave me support and encouragement. As did my family – with love and shelter thrown in. And Rex Audley, my collaborator in so many ventures, provided far more than illustrations. It would have been a different book without him and far less fun to write.

One word of apology. 'He', of course, also represents 'she'; 'him' and 'his' also represent 'her'.

1 Structure and Execution

I was walking along a highway in the Arizona desert. Fifty miles' radius of very little. The only vehicle was in front of me. A camera truck. It cruised slowly as I spoke to it.

I had a page of commentary to deliver. I tried to forget the sun, the faces of the crew, the position of the mike. I tried to remember the pace and gestures we had rehearsed and above all the words I had written six weeks earlier in Los Angeles, to be spoken in the desert, as if I had just thought of them.

We finished the take. The director was pleased. We did one more – for fun – and the crew got ready to move on.

While they packed I re-read the script. I had done that page in virtually one take yet there had been shots of two to three lines which had demanded eight, nine, a dozen attempts to get right. Why? Unaccountable off days? Or something in the text itself? What made it easier to remember? I examined the structure of my script. The page was *put together*. The argument was logical. It sounded right, colloquial, the way I would talk. I compared it with some of the passages I had had difficulty with during the shoot. A few I had needed to alter before I felt happy with them.

Then the penny dropped.

> More important than delivery was structure. *Before I put it across I needed to put it together.* The better I put it together the more easily I could put it across.

But what were the signs of a 'good' structure? Were there rules? After all colloquial speech seems to come naturally to everybody and professional writers who create dialogue seem merely to echo natural cadences and forms. Wasn't it simply a knack?

And yet when I thought of the tedious lectures I had endured at college, the learned papers, the professional discourses and subsequently the commercial presentations I had attended, I realised that though the majority of educated people can write something to be read, they can seldom write something to be heard. Indeed, they are generally unaware that there is a difference. Papers are 'read' to learned societies. The speaker pores over his text. The audience is afforded a view of the crown of his head. And as for visual aids ...

This book attempts to teach the reader how to present. It is addressed to anyone who has to stand up in front of an audience, especially in a commercial context, and persuade it to do something. Change its mind, think again, think in a new way, accept a totally new idea, maybe even go out and buy something.

A presentation aims to get a thought out of your head into somebody else's and thereby change that person.

That definition holds whether you are a lecturer, marketing director, chairperson of the board, a government official talking to the media or a priest before his flock.

Your audience may be deluded into believing that the purpose of your presentation is to entertain, divert, inspire or get across ideas and information. Indeed you may even be deluded yourself. But stop to think. What do you want the audience (that man in the third row) to think, believe, feel, *do* as a result of what you're saying?

If you can answer that you'll know that it's something tangible. If you can't then maybe you should not be making a presentation (or maybe you need this book).

After all the audience is there for a purpose. It may have invited you to address it. It may have paid money to hear you. It has accepted you as a spokesman or an authority or even an expert. And, until you prove otherwise, it gives you the benefit of the doubt. It also assumes that you can present, that you have afforded them the courtesy of preparing your material, of researching your audience, of rehearsing and timing your text.

> To present is to enter into a contract with the audience.

Few presenters, alas, treat presentation that professionally.

Not that they don't worry about it. Indeed they are so successful at worrying about it that they fail once and never do it again. Others simply repeat their failures believing there are a few natural presenters and the rest. Good presenters have a knack, a gift.

Proficiency of speaking is *not* a gift. It can be learned. But the learning begins not with delivery but with structure. Before you can learn to put it across you must learn to put it together.

er...er...er...

Proficiency of speaking is NOT a gift

It is not easy.

The restraints on time, the ordering of material, the relationship of what is said to what is shown by means of visual aids ... these are major barriers. But more dangerous is the delusion that because anything written can be spoken, therefore anything spoken can be understood.

There are other barriers too which we'll examine – for example, the attention span of the audience and the conflicting claims upon that attention.

Cicero knew how difficult life is for the presenter. 'In an orator we must demand the subtlety of the magician, the thoughts of the philosopher, a diction almost poetic, a lawyer's memory, a tragedian's voice, and the bearing almost of the consummate actor.'[1]

But that's rhetoric, people say. As a nation we are cautious of oratory, of the well-turned phrase. Rhetoric is commonly a pejorative term. Plato's definition, however, is moderate. In *Phaedrus* he has Socrates define it as 'a method of influencing men's minds by means of words, whether the words are spoken in a court of law or before some other body or in private conversation'.[2] Nevertheless modern commentators place rhetoric in antithesis to the facts.

But facts matter to the presenter. As much to the good presenter as to the indifferent one. Indeed they matter so much to the former that he arranges his facts into as effective a communication as possible and practises the means of delivering that communication to ensure that the facts reach their intended destination in the condition in which they left his mind. How those facts are assembled, how they are organized for the audience, i.e., *structure*, we deal with in the first section of this book – 'Put It Together'.

How those arranged facts are delivered, what might be called '*execution*', is the subject of the second section – 'Put It Across'.

Do not, however, equate structure and execution with matter and manner. The 'what' and the 'how' are important at *both* stages. The style in which the facts are assembled contributes meaningfully to the structure: and the manner of delivery provides additional matter, communicates additional 'facts', during the execution.

Structure and execution then (**PIT** and **PIA**) constitute the body of the book. This is prefaced by a short reminder of the basics of communication.

However, before that we need to answer one question – should you *write* a *speech*?

2 Write the Speech

Speaking comes easily – at least in private. We put our thoughts together seemingly without effort. People had been speaking some fifty thousand years before they invented script. Writing is humanity's greatest technological achievement. It has to be consciously learned. Speaking seems to be learned unconsciously by imitating the sounds of other people. Speaking begins, in the child, with the making of analogies. Then the child constructs sentences by adapting other sentences. It puts them together. It connects. It makes progress. It develops thoughts.

If colloquial speech is 'natural' to us why

(1)   bother to prepare a speech apart from making a few notes?
(2)   is it difficult to write a speech that comes across well?
(3)   not simply dictate a speech into a tape recorder, transcribe it and subsequently read the text?

This chapter attempts to answer these questions.

My position, however, is absolutely clear. *A presenter should always write his speech.*

Note: That does *not*

(1)   mean *reading* the speech, or
(2)   exclude speaking from notes.

Unless you are a trained, experienced presenter do not attempt to give a speech from notes without first having written the speech in full.

Not writing a speech but making a few notes and speaking 'off the cuff' (where the notes were concealed when men had cuffs you could write on) is an art form perfected by one presenter in a hundred. A few speakers can perform the trick without any notes at all. A. J. P. Taylor is one. Mark Twain gave the impression of speaking extemporaneously though he admitted that many of his 'spontaneous' speeches took him three weeks of preparation.

You may be able to ad-lib in the friendly environment of your home, or even in front of a few colleagues, but a sea change takes place once the audience has filled the strange hall. (Indeed a half-filled hall may be even more intimidating.)

Furthermore, the length of time you need to fill may daunt you if you have not first written the speech and timed it. You may find it difficult to estimate time as it passes and even if you have constructed the shape of the speech – in your mind and in your notes – you may find that ad-libbing leads you into side roads.

Some you pursue willingly – since you know your way back. Others you stumble upon, mistake for the path you first mapped. And even if you know your way back it's doubtful if your audience shares your powers of navigation.

Colloquial speech is natural. But is natural speech the best means of communicating what you want to say? The trick is not to be natural but to *appear* natural. Artifice is inevitable. The whole business of getting up and addressing an audience in a strange place over a set period of time is hardly a natural event.

Besides, if you have ever listened to natural speech – or especially, had to read it – over a long period, you will know how boring, repetitive, shapeless and infuriating it is. You would hardly wish that fate upon your audience. Nobody speaks fluently, becomes articulate, without practice and training. And part of that training consists of structuring the material, putting it together, and shaping it – not for the eye, but for the ear.

But wouldn't *dictating* the speech guarantee that? Dictation ensures that the meaning is reasonably clear – if only because the act of speaking your thoughts does help to articulate them. The only way you can get them across to someone else is first to get them across to yourself, to speak your thoughts.

But you pay a penalty. Or rather the audience pays it. Dictated text bears signs of sloppiness, repetition and, to adapt Orwell, ready-made phrases taking over from thought.

Dictation serves well enough for business letters. But even here you will spot the untidy sentence, the repeated sentence form, the cliché sentiment.

Dictating for practice is useful. Speaking extempore is good exercise. But you must – as with all good exercise – spot and correct your faults.

'By speaking men become speakers.' To which Cicero responded that it is equally true that by speaking badly men become bad speakers.[1]

And what do audiences mean by a bad speech? 'He didn't say much and it went on too long', perhaps. Two dangers for the presenter who dictates.

If the presenter said little how could it have gone on too long? But we know what's meant. What content there was was badly presented. A good structure (**PIT**) might have transformed that content into an effective presentation. If a slim thought is expressed badly, or elaborated on or repeated, then its cutting edge is usually blunted.

But probably the thought needed working at by the presenter. And dictation – speaking aloud – is not an effective way of doing that. Speaking aloud may help you articulate your thoughts – i.e. present them in a clear way to a listener (the first of whom is yourself). But speaking aloud is less successful in helping you think those thoughts in the first place or build upon them to create further thoughts.

The reason is obvious. Speech is a rapid process. Sound is transitory. As Walter Ong says, 'All sensation takes place in time but sound has a special relationship to time unlike that of the other fields that register in human sensation. Sound exists only when it is going out of existence. It is not simply perishable but essentially evanescent. When I pronounce the word "permanence", by the time I get to the "nence" the "perma" is gone and has to be gone.'[2]

Writing, on the other hand, occupies the mind ten times longer than speaking. Therefore it can better deal with analytical thought.

If speech helps you articulate your thoughts, writing can in addition also help you clarify them, improve them, augment them ... reject them. It provides the time for you to be analytic – and provides the pen and paper (or the keyboard and VDU).

Writing helps you plan. A well thought-out plan has been described as 'the shortest route from the purpose to the goal'.[3] The presenter must determine the shape of what is to come. The writer of course does the same thing. 'The more clearly he perceives the shape', says Strunk in one of the best and shortest books on writing style, 'the better are his chances of success'.[4]

The presenter needs to plan even more than the writer because whereas the writer's audience can go back on the material and, if necessary compensate for the writer's shortcomings, the presenter's audience will not have the time or the information to adjust the material. Indeed whereas bad planning in the written text may result merely in inconvenience, in the spoken text it may well result in total incomprehension.

'The best speakers', says Barry Turner, 'are always in control. They know where they are and where they are going. To do this requires planning.'[5]

And planning does not happen spontaneously. You need to discipline yourself. Writing the speech is a disciplining process. It shows up any faults in your reasoning, reveals the half thought, distinguishes the true from the false.

Only by writing your speech can you properly structure your argument. And for most of us only by writing our speech can we make sure that we pin down exactly what we are thinking.

Sloppy language is evidence of sloppy thought. 'What a man cannot state', said a Ministry of Education report in 1921, 'he does not perfectly know, and, consequently, the inability to put his thoughts into words sets a boundary to his thoughts.'[6]

But, as has been suggested, writing in full has another advantage over dictation and note taking in preparing our speech. It transforms what we have to say. In Ong's words 'it enlarges the potentiality of language'.[7]

Writing is a more creative act than talking. By committing our thoughts to space we can restructure those thoughts. Writing can help give those thoughts a body, a dimension. They become building tools.

Writing makes thoughts tangible. So even abstract concepts are manageable. Herein lies a danger for the speaker since the text has to be transformed back to a spoken form and made comprehensible to a listener rather than a reader.

But this is the case with *all* written speeches.

The manuscript you prepare is not the manuscript you deliver.

The former we shall call a text. The latter we shall term a script.

The **text** is what you write.
The **script** is what you speak.

The bad presenter writes a text and speaks that. The good one writes a text and converts it into a script. The exceptional ones manage to write a script first go.

We shall examine the difference between text and script extensively in Chapter 17. But whichever we write neither of them should be *read* to an audience (though obviously a read-out text, i.e. a manuscript written for reading will sound worse than a read-out script).

A read-out speech is a contradiction in terms and an insult to the audience. The members of the audience are being treated, at best, as observers of a ritual. Their presence is virtually ignored and their participation manifestly denied.

Both speaker and listener would derive greater benefit by having the text printed and distributed to the audience. Charles James Fox was probably right in asserting that 'a speech that reads well is a damned bad one when spoken'.[8]

Moreover, the text actually creates a barrier between the speaker and his audience. The presenter locks himself in his text. The physical paper in front of him, instead of being a means (i.e. an aid to communication) becomes an end in itself (i.e. the thing already communicated).

No – the rule is *write* a *text*. Transform it into the script and *deliver the script* – maybe turning the script into *notes*.

The more experienced you get the more your initial text will resemble a script. But at this stage don't worry if the transformation has to be gone through – just as long as you appreciate and can recognize the difference between a text and a script.

Alistair Cooke may give the impression that he is speaking spontaneously. He in fact writes every word of each *Letter from America*. But Cooke writes like a good talker.

And audiences would prefer that you write like a good talker than talk like a good writer.

Write. Write. Write.

But make sure you *write to be heard*.

Roman orators practised both arts – speaking and writing. Indeed if they had not written their speeches it would have been impossible to construct the laws of rhetoric which in turn made them better orators. As Ong points out, 'writing did not reduce orality but enhanced it, making it possible to organise the "principle" or constituents of oratory into a scientific art'.[9]

Roman orators practised both arts – speaking and writing

'I have come to inter Caesar not to eulogise him...'

'Take time for consideration', Cicero taught, 'and speak better prepared and more carefully. Write as much as possible. The pen is the best and most eminent author and teacher of eloquence'.[10]

Cicero knew that the act of writing helped create the speech. 'All thoughts and expressions which are the most brilliant in their several kinds, must needs flow up in succession to the point of our pen'.[11]

Writing also helps us put it together: 'then too the actual marshalling and arrangement of words is made perfect in the course of writing'.[12]

Cicero concludes this sentence with the rider 'in a rhythm and measure proper to oratory as distinct from poetry'.[13] We would say 'in a language proper to speech as distinct from literature'.

The text has to be made script. Otherwise the full meaning may be lost. The script has to sound 'natural', as if the thought and the speech have been born simultaneously. Clearly this is unlikely but the audience is willing to suspend disbelief – provided the artifice is professionally executed. For art, as Longinus reminds us, 'is perfect only when it looks like nature'.[14] The art that hides art. The three weeks of sweat behind Mark Twain's 'spontaneity'. The dramatist praised for natural dialogue is the craftsman artificially creating the illusion of natural dialogue: just as the accomplished author or poet can create the sense of disorder by the most careful attention to order.[4]

Order is all – the order of thought, content, and language.

Speaking cannot impose order. Writing can.

Write the speech.

3 Basic Communication

Before we start putting it together let us remind ourselves of the basics of communication. The material is probably familiar to you. However, the context may not be. Re-examine the 'laws' in the context of presentation.

The traditional model is simple.[1]

Definition: communication concerns 'who says what to whom along what channels and with what effect.'[2]. There are several other definitions, none as practical or as comprehensive.

The model involves two participants: a transmitter and a receiver — in our context, a presenter and an audience.

I choose the word participant deliberately because the audience takes part. Indeed the individual member of the audience is never a passive recipient. He affects the message (quantitatively and qualitatively) as much as the transmitter. He can choose what he wants to receive. He can, by his actions or lack of attention, significantly diminish the signal which is being sent (e.g. by doodling with his pencil on a pad). He can also considerably enhance the signal (e.g. by using that pencil to make key notes).

Communication does not consist of a 'communicator' and a 'communicatee'. Though many mass communicators would like it so. The language of marketing betrays a one-way view of the process. The receiver is the 'target audience'. Now you don't exchange messages with targets. You try to *hit* them. The language is full of military borrowings – campaign, plan of attack, burst, rifleshot, etc.

All communication is dialogue.
Even if you can't receive the response.

Communication is not the firing of signals into the mind of a passive receiver but the *exchange* of signals between two participants. Even the most passive receiver, the television viewer in the armchair, reacts to the screen. The performer (and writer and director) must plan for that reaction, must prepare the material for some bounce back of the signal. Confirmation of that return signal may be difficult to achieve. Research, viewing figures, complaints, discussions may tell the team whether or not the reaction was as anticipated. But that is a delayed signal. No wonder television people encourage the studio audience. The presenter, of course, always has a studio audience and the benefit of immediate reaction. The bad presenter is often surprised by it. The good presenter tries to anticipate it. As we shall see in the next chapter, the good presentation text is never a monologue. *It is one half of a dialogue.*

Communication is two-way.

Communicare is a Latin word meaning 'to share'.

'Human communication', says Ong, 'is never one-way. It calls for response. The context we choose, the way we shape it, is determined by an anticipated response.'[3]

The same approach is adopted by the sensitive marketing man. He begins at the end — with the response. What does he want the respondent to think, feel, believe, do — as a result of the communication?

The transmitter must think like the receiver. It's the only way to start.

The key constituents of the communication model are these:

Transmitter
Receiver
Message
Encoder
Decoder

The **transmitter** thinks of a **message**. Perfect transmission is achieved if the message reaches the **receiver**'s mind in the identical form in which it left the transmitter. The return message from the receiver should tell the transmitter if this is the case.

It sounds simple. But you know how the simplest messages – instructions to your family or office colleagues – can go awry. Communication which is meant to get things done often renders people ineffective. Nothing gets done. The wrong things get done.

Whose fault?

The onus is on the transmitter. Always. It must be since he is instigating the communication.

How does he do this? By **encoding** his message.

Encoding? If this sounds a bit rich for your blood – after all doesn't it simply mean turning your thoughts into normal everyday language? – please bear with me.

Yes – encoding *is* simply that. And that is where the trouble starts.

Transmitters forget that they are talking in code.

Language is a code. Let us imagine two primitive men in a forest coming upon a small four-legged animal barking and wagging its tail.

'Dog!' utters the first man.
'Dog?' replies the second, puzzled.
'Dog!' repeats the first, pointing to the animal.

Oral language has been augmented. The monosyllabic sound has been registered. The sound 'dog' is a signifier for the thing signified (i.e. the animal).

Fifty thousand years later comes a technological breakthrough. Somebody writes the letters 'd-o-g' as a means of pictorially signifying the oral signifier.

The written word 'dog' is a secondary code, a visual code for the oral code for the actual thing.

The fact that we use spoken and written words instinctively should not detract us from thinking of language as a code. In fact most of the problems of poor communication arise from this *unthinking* use of language.

Think of language as a code, however, and something very significant happens.

You think of the receiver. The **decoder**. Because unless the receiver knows the code he cannot decode it. *Communicare* means to share. Unless there is 'shared meaning' there *is* no communication.

Write the word 'code' on the cover of your script to remind you to make sure that you and your audience share your meaning.

If the code is common, your chances of getting through, though considerably improved, are not guaranteed. Other factors are at work diminishing the integrity of the signal you are transmitting.

With luck and good planning you can find out. Through **feedback**.

Feedback takes many forms. Some are obvious, e.g. questions, applause, laughter, attentive silence. Some signs you need to interpret, e.g. the way individuals sit, look, rub their faces (body language).

Signs of impatience and boredom are easy to detect – shuffling papers, looking at a watch, shifting positions.

Signs of boredom are easy to detect

Some are ambiguous. How do you know if your compulsive note taker isn't writing a love letter?

Feedback – a return of your signal which indicates whether your message has been received and, more importantly, *understood*.

If feedback tells you both you can progress. If the former, you can adjust. If it tells you differently at least you know you have a problem. But if you have no feedback at all you will not know you have a problem until it is too late to do anything about it.

The problem may not be of your own making. There could be factors outside your control diminishing the integrity of your signal. The sound system may have picked up the local taxi rank (this happened to me). However, the onus is on the transmitter. You must prepare.

Let us call what you want to transmit **sound**. Then – in the terminology of the communication scientist – what diminishes it is **noise**.

Noise is of three sorts – and no presentation, no presenter, is immune.

Channel noise means there is something wrong with the medium of communication.

The taxi rank we quoted. No mike. A hoarse voice. Adenoids. Too much illumination whilst showing slides. A dirty slide. A wrong slide. The rattling of cutlery and crockery in the anteroom. Restricted viewing of the screen. The speaker's mannerisms. Etc., etc.

To list the things which could go wrong would only depress you. Better then to break them down into those items you can *prevent*, those you can *check* up on before the event and those you can merely *pray* won't happen.

A speaker's mannerisms
constitute
CHANNEL NOISE

Code noise means using a word or visual in one sense and being received in another or not being received at all. Common faults are professional jargon, technical terms, foreign words and the use of ambiguous phrases.

But the main culprit is language which is meant to be read rather than heard. Why, when I say 'patio door', should my audience hear the name of an Irish singer?

Unless the text becomes a script, code noise will be deafening.

Of all the forms of noise it is the one the presenter can do most about, and in the privacy of his own room.

Psychological noise means that there is something unsettling in the relationship between the transmitter and the receiver.

The presenter's manner of delivery (see Chapter 23) may be fighting his message. He may appear haughty, superior, too intellectual or patronizing. His accent may brand him as cultured or an alien. His seeming aggressiveness (probably an overcompensation for nerves) may annoy. The chairperson's introduction may have set the wrong tone and the speaker spends the next few minutes living it down. Blood sugar could be low. Lunch could be near. The meeting could have gone on too long.

Psychological noise is the hardest for the presenter to deal with. Nevertheless, the onus is still on the transmitter. He must check his manner of delivery. He must research the audience. He must familiarize himself with the context of the presentation – i.e. the physical context and the emotional. He must try to estimate the atmosphere which has been created and which his appearance is likely to affect and be affected by.

PSYCHOLOGICAL NOISE

Haughty, superior,
intellectual and
patronising

The categories of noise often overlap. A phrase (code) may carry with it an implication of, say, intellectualism (psychological) irrespective of delivery. A speaker using a Latin tag with a non-classical audience could be guilty of both code and psychological noise. And if he also had a code id his doze ... channel noise as well.

I expect by now you may have misgivings about making presentations. But take heart. Appreciating the problem is half way to solving it. Too many presenters are so thick-skinned they are not aware of the problem. And, if they are conscious of audience reaction, they expect the audience to compensate for any fault in the material or the delivery.

As I frequently point out
to my wife, 'Linguam
compescere, virtus non
minima est'...

Code AND psychological noise

The good presenter knows that communication is an exchange, that the meaning of the transaction is not contained only within the intended message (i.e. the typescript in front of him).

As Hawkes says, 'a good deal of what is communicated derives from the context, the code and the means of contact. "Meaning" in short resides in the *total* act of communication.'[4]

That 'total' act includes the additional messages which the presenter's 'body language' is transmitting. These cues can reinforce and enhance the intended message; or negate or contradict them. The power of non-verbal communication must never be underestimated. For some receivers the nonverbal may be the real one and the verbal message so much noise.

Also within the total act is the luggage which the receiver brings with him to the transaction. How he sees himself, his needs, values, attributes; his culture ... all can affect the way the receiver receives. The identical information can be interpreted quite differently by two apparently similar people. Communication is a difficult process of finding common ground between transmitter and receiver.

- How can you, the sender, reduce the complexities?

- What can you prevent?

- What can you check?

- What must you leave to prayer?

If you want to enhance sound and reduce noise you must first discover the likely source of noise.

NOISE can originate in

i) Text	iii) Equipment	v) Audience
ii) Delivery	iv) Room	

You can deal with *all* of the above – though with decreasing ability.

The toughest assignment then is the *audience*, which is where we start to **put it together**.

4   Think Like a Listener

If the message of Chapter 2 is *write like a good talker*, and you have read Chapter 3, then it will come as no surprise to find that the message of Chapter 4 is

Think like a listener

think like a listener.

Aristotle divided the concerns of the orator into three: the subject matter, the purpose and the audience. Two thousand years later the majority of speakers pay least attention to the third.

Maybe people feel uneasy beginning at the end. Adam Smith warned manufacturers 'consumption is the sole end and purpose of all production: and the interest of the producer ought to be attended to, only so far as it may be necessary for promoting that of the consumer'. Yet two hundred years later companies proclaim 'customer focus' in terms usually associated with 'Eureka!'

Thinking like a customer is for some reason a difficult task for the manufacturer. And yet he spends as much of his life being a customer as a maker. Asked to criticize a company – in a field other than his own – he will usually speak as a customer, satisfied or otherwise, and will have firm opinions on that company's service and how to improve it. Yet applying that experience to his own business, looking at his company's products and service from the standpoint of the person who pays his salary, the customer, is a task he can rarely perform unaided, much to the relief of consultancies and the market research industry.

When Hamlet advises the players who have come to Elsinore to perform before the court he speaks as a paying customer who has suffered in the past. He is offended by fellows tearing a passion to tatters. His comments are relevant to today's presenter.

> suit the action to the word, the word to the action ... anything overdone is from the purpose of playing, whose end both, both at the first and now, was and is to hold, as 'twere, the mirror up to nature.

But *Hamlet* is a mirror too – in which the actors, by becoming spectators, view their own shortcomings. Today's presenter of course has the benefit of videotape.

You cannot begin to prepare a presentation without understanding communication and the part played by the receiver. Think of one of the simplest messages which pass between people on and off platforms, namely the joke. What happens when a listener does not react? What does he say? Either 'I don't get it' or 'I don't think that's funny'. In both cases he has taken part. In the first he has tried and failed, the connection hasn't been made. In the second he has succeeded but the connection has revealed, for him, no significant incongruity.

Try this:

> 'Waiter there's a needle in my soup.'
> 'No sir, that's a typographical error. Noodle.'

(The world is divided into two sorts of people: those who think that's funny and accountants.)

A joke is a joke precisely because the receiver *participates*. The presenter must think like the listener and encourage the listener to participate.

Participation, of course, is not confined to jokes. The member of the audience has five senses. Three you hope are dormant and two (sight and hearing) you are engaging. But more importantly you need to engage his brain. *What is he likely to be thinking as you speak?* What would *you* be thinking? How would you react to somebody telling *you* that?

Communicare means to share. The audience must share in the performance, in the event, in the *activity*.

A presentation is not a sit-back but a *sit-up* medium.

A presentation is not a sit-back but a sit-up medium

It is easier to get the audience to share your opinion if you get it to share in the work.

To repeat, a speech should be written not as a monologue but as one half of a dialogue. From time to time in your text insert a comment or question from the listener. You must know what response you require – the overall response at the end and the individual responses during the course of your presentation.

You want the audience's agreement and subsequent action but you have to earn it. Only despots require the unthinking acceptance of an audience.

Occasionally you might deliberately provoke an audience into disagreement, into questioning what you say. You could plant an inconsistency and hope the audience spots it. (The master presenter can do this. It is dangerous for the beginner.) These techniques provide light and shade. They may entertain, amuse, surprise the audience. More importantly they *keep the audience busy.*

At the end of the first act in the theatre bar you can tell how well the play is going by the buzz of the crowd. 'They are buzzy because we kept them busy.' (Old theatrical maxim I've just invented.)

Incidentally don't be scared by all these theatrical references. A performance *is* theatre. You forget that at your peril. *Live* theatre. So it loses much of its potential if you rely on too much filmed material. So it benefits if you regard your script not as a monologue but as *one half of a dialogue.* Dialogue is much more *dramatic.*

Obviously before you start to write you must learn as much as you can about the audience.

(1) How many?
(2) Sex breakdown? Age range? Status (social and financial)? Educational background? Racial background?
(3) What links them – if anything? Is it a homogeneous or diverse group?
(4) What are their expectations? Why are they there? What were they told?
(5) What do they know of the subject?
(6) What do they know of the presenter?
(7) How important is the subject to their professional or social lives?
(8) 'Do they come here often?' (e.g. are presentations part of their normal fare? Are they sick to the teeth of this subject? Have they preconceived ideas?)
(9) What mood are they likely to be in? (This may depend on the business they're in, the timing of the speech, recent events, etc. This has to be monitored right up to the moment of delivery.)

And finally, the almost intangible...

(10) What is the personality of the audience?

You will only begin to know the answer to question (10) on the day – let's hope not too late into your speech. Try to speak to *some* members of the audience before you speak to all of them. Try to gauge their expectations, needs, values, goals, standards, interests. All, as we have noted, have an effect upon 'the way the input is received and interpreted'.

You may discover that you have a hostile or at best a negative audience. Just as well then that you have prepared a dialogue full of unspoken questions. It may now be necessary actually to *voice* those questions, to put both sides of the argument. You should be prepared for questions at the end of your presentation. But in the words of Antony Jay, 'do not wrestle when you should use judo'. [1] 'A presentation is very rarely the time to show people that their strongly held beliefs are erroneous. The most you can do is accept their beliefs but show them that they have drawn the wrong conclusions. Intellectual judo is using the force of the other man's opinions and prejudices to win your argument.' [2]

Of course if you can find out why the audience is negative you will be in a better position to connect with it. I once gave a new business presentation recommending a course of action to a potential client without having discovered that a competitive company had in fact been employed in a similar capacity some three years before with unfortunate results.

Finally, research into your audience may reveal a 'hidden agenda'. You or your company may have been invited to speak on a specific topic to serve some purpose beyond the assumed intention.

Your seeming objectivity (e.g. as an outside expert) may be being used by a faction within the audience (e.g. a company or association) to help its case in an internal argument or, even, battle for power. That is why question (7) on the *importance* of the subject is so . . . important.

In their justly celebrated *The Reader over Your Shoulder: Handbook for Writers of English Prose* Robert Graves and Alan Hodge suggest 'that whenever anyone sits down to write he should imagine a crowd of his prospective readers . . . looking over his shoulder.'

You should imagine a listener in the chair opposite. Let's call him Eric.

Eric

You know what it is like being a listener if the speaker hasn't engaged your brain. How hungry you feel or thirsty or itchy. How you would prefer to be *doing something.*

You should make sure that the audience is doing something. Preferably something connected with your presentation. After all it has come prepared to listen. As Antony Jay says, 'at the end of the first ten minutes they should be wanting to know'.[4] (That's why the *beginning* of your script is so important.)

If the audience is equipped with pen and paper make sure you encourage it to use them.

Think like the listener. As one yourself do you try to make notes? Do you look for the structure of the speech during the presentation?

Do you write down key points? What encourages you to pick up your pen? A novel phrase? A new idea? A reference you can pursue later? A nugget?

Re-read your text for nuggets. Better still ask a colleague. He may find a nugget in something you yourself take for granted.

There is one device which usually encourages the listener to lift up his pen, particularly early on in the presentation – a short list.

'There are only three solutions to the problem . . .'

There are two (see what I mean?) advantages to this approach.

(1) Written down, the outline and argument are easier to follow.
(2) The listener has something which he himself can subsequently *use.*

Note how often pens are raised whenever a speaker enumerates. But don't overdo it.

Involve the audience. From the beginning. When you have their attention – for free. Thereafter it has to be *earned.*

Studies of the 'attention curve' show how attention starts high then declines gradually and picks up when the end is in sight. You needed no psychologist to tell you that. It merely confirmed your own experiences as a listener. But, I beseech you, benefit from your own experience.

(1) Utilize the first few minutes. State key points.
(2) Engage the audience during the 'long middle' by keeping it busy.
(3) Utilize the last few minutes. Sum up – preferably in one memorable phrase.

The listener is kept busy by being made to think, by working something out, by physically doing something.

Remember the old Chinese adage:

I hear I forget.
I see I remember.
I do I understand.

As a member of an audience you remember best what you actually take part in. A joke you *take part* in. You close the gap, make the connection. A joke is not a joke if it has to be explained.

As a presenter invite participation. Ask Eric in the chair opposite to interrupt you as you write your presentation. If all he says is 'why?' that will help. And when you answer let him ask why again. And again. That may drive you mad. It may on the other hand reveal woolly thinking. You may as a result replace 'ready-made phrases' with genuine thoughts.

Not that the irritating Eric opposite is merely a thinking machine. You must allow for both the rational and the nonrational in the audience. My favourite estate agents were called Reason and Tickle. If they hadn't actually lived on the south coast I surely would have invented them. No communication is entirely reason or entirely tickle. The presenter has to judge the proportion according to Aristotle's trinity – the subject matter, the purpose, and the audience.

And what goes for the presenter goes for the advertiser, the street market trader and the orator. Here is Cicero, through the mouth of Antonius, beginning at the end, thinking of the listener:

Now nothing in oratory, Catullus, is more important than to win for the orator the favour of his hearer, and to have the latter so effective as to be swayed by something resembling a mental impulse or emotion, rather than by judgement or deliberation. For men decide more problems by hate or love or lust or rage or sorrow or joy or hope or fear or illusion or some other inward emotion than by rationality or authority or any legal standard, or judicial precedent or statute.[5]

If you think like a listener and you have done your homework then you will communicate in terms of the listener's experience.

Putting it together isn't simply the art of relating one thought to another but relating your thoughts to the listener's experience and knowledge.

And if that knowledge is inadequate? Then maybe you have to supplement it during your presentation.

C. P. Scott, the editor of the *Manchester Guardian*, advised his reporters: 'Never underestimate the intelligence of your readers. Always underestimate their knowledge.' It is perfect advice. Your audience may not know the things you expect them to (or indeed believe they should). So it may be up to you to tell them. But if you observe the first half of Scott's equation – and don't underestimate their intelligence – you will convey that information in such a way as *not to patronize* your audience.

To begin at the end. You want your audience to act (the 'target response'). But before they can act they must remember. Before they remember they must believe, or at least be prepared to give you the benefit of the doubt. Before they can believe they must understand.

Making them understand is your responsibility.

The onus is on the transmitter.

'The sender must be in the receiver position before he can send.'[6]

5   Purpose and Point

The one lesson in public speaking we've all learned is:

(1) Tell them what you're going to tell them.
(2) Tell them.
(3) Tell them what you have told them.

Good advice. A basic way of putting it together. However...

do you have anything *to* tell them?

You know the one about the small boy and the sermon? He tells his father after church that the vicar has given a sermon on sin. 'What did he say?' asks his father. 'He was against it', replies the boy.

Well, do you have anything to say? Presumably. Otherwise why did you accept the invitation to speak? Or why did you invite all those people to attend? Will you leave your audience with anything more focused than the vicar did?

Focus is crucial. Apply it initially to the particular term you use concerning the first of Aristotle's trinity – subject matter.

What's the '*subject*' of your presentation? 'Information technology in Britain today.' That's broad. Try another word. Focus.

What's your '*theme*'? 'Not enough attention is being paid to educating the non-user.' That's better. Focus some more.

What's your '*point*'?

If you can't answer that – if you don't, in the jargon of the journalist, have an 'angle' – maybe you shouldn't accept the invitation to speak.

Of course the invitation may be accompanied by a request for a title.

Progammes have to be printed, audiences attracted. How will you respond – with a subject, a theme or a point? The title may act as a catalyst or a restraint; a subject we'll pursue in the next chapter.

Focusing brings us from the broad to the narrow, the fuzzy to the sharp.

A single point.

If you don't have one there is obviously a problem. There is a problem – though less obvious – if you have several. If you don't have anything to say you shouldn't start. If you have too many things to say you may not be able to stop.

Any presentation should be capable of being summed up in one key sentence. You may want your audience to remember several points but they should all be subsumed under one single central point. And recall of that single point should bring with it recall of all the subsidiary points. This clearly has implications for how you structure your speech but no speech can be structured until that single point is determined.

How to come to the point?

One way is to begin with the purpose of your presentation. If you have decided upon your target response it will be easier to decide your central point. Be careful that you don't confuse 'purpose' with 'point'. The purpose of your presentation is, say, to convince the borough council of the need to spend more on the public library facilities. The point you make could be any or all of the following:

(1) The stock of books is inadequate.
(2) Many of the books are out of date.
(3) Demand for the useful books exceeds the supply.
(4) Half of the useful books are damaged.
(5) Compared with other similar councils, library funding is niggardly.

You now have to decide which one of those is the most important or whether one can justify the whole presentation; or, in the likely event that you want to get across *all* of the points, how you can link them in a single point, a central idea which will achieve your purpose.

The single point must subsume all the others. (That will depend upon how you structure the argument.) The single point is essential.

It provides the *point of entry*.

If you will accept the uncomfortable simile, it is like a dumdum bullet which expands upon impact.

You may choose one major point and attach the others to it. You may concoct a slogan or catch phrase which captures the essence not only of your argument but also of your passion. For example, 'Don't turn the library into a museum', or 'Books are the tools to shape our future – invest now.'

The great advantage of a slogan, of course, is that it is both an encapsulation and an injunction. As such it pays homage to Aristotle. It achieves the *purpose* of the presentation by summing up the *subject matter* in a direct address to the *audience*.

But whether or not you manage to create a slogan it is crucial to focus on a single point. One of the virtues of a good presenter is single-mindedness. You can't achieve this unless you have a point to be single-minded about! And unless you have a point how do you know if you are ever off it?

One single point – that's the aim irrespective of the size or length of the presentation. A multi-screen Wembley Conference Centre extravaganza or an across-the-table, back-of-an-envelope exposition to a lunch guest.

When you start to write the text put that single point in front of you. Use one of those yellow post-it notes and stick it on the wall or desk.

And once the presentation is written read it through with that single point in front of you. Does every page contribute to the argument? If not why not? Is that a tangent? What purpose does it serve? Is that joke in there because you feel sorry for the audience? Empathizing with the listener is admirable. But if you tell a joke which augments or illustrates your point the laugh affords not just relief but *insight*.

As we've seen it's easy to stray from your point. Better than a side road is a minor detour. Better than a tangent which only just touches is an overlapping circle. Overlapping circles *connect*. Tangents don't.

Presentations, we have agreed, take place in a commercial context. So maybe an analogy with advertising is valid. Any advertisement has to be judged on at least four criteria:

Visibility	Identity	Promise	Single-mindedness

– **VIPS** for short. (I read that in a book I wrote.[1])

- *Visibility* – does it stand out?
- *Identity* – is the brand name registered?
- *Promise* – what's the benefit for the potential customer?
- *Single-mindedness* – is everything in the ad pointing the same way (i.e. helping to put across the promise to the recipient)?

It is not difficult to apply those same criteria to your presentation.

- *Visibility* – does it stand out? (i.e. from the rest of the conference? From competitive presentations – past, present and future?)
- *Identity* – is your name (and/or that of your company or organization) firmly locked in to the message?
- *Promise* – what do you want the listener to take away with him and *use* (preferably to his and your mutual benefit)?
- *Single-mindedness* – is everything in the presentation pointing the same way?

You should assess the finished text against those criteria. Better still, bear them in mind when you start.

However, it may happen that you cannot decide on your single point (or even whether you have any point) until you start upon the project. Indeed in the next chapter I'll urge you not to wait for inspiration. But if you don't have a point *you must have a purpose*. You cannot possibly enter upon a presentation unless and until you have a purpose.

'A screenwriter', says William Goldman, 'should on a fly-leaf write his intent. Because sometimes during shooting people get lost.'[2]

Hardly surprising. During a presentation too. What with the equipment and crew and ancillary characters plus the audience it is very easy to get lost. But there is no excuse for getting lost in your own study when the text is still a text and you can check every line against, if not your point, then certainly your purpose.

'The rhetorician', says the *Encyclopaedia Britannica*, '…regards the text as the embodiment of an intention .   .   . He knows also of the structure of a piece of discourse. The way its major points fit together is profoundly a result of its intention.'[3]

It's time we made a start on – embodying our intention.

6 Assembly

Ready. Aim. Fire!

You have a purpose. Now begin. And frankly it does not matter where. Start anywhere – but start. Do not put it off because you do not have an idea, let alone the *point*. A trial page or two will provide an idea. A few isolated notes may suddenly connect. The copywriter finds that writing the text provides the headline. Or perhaps a better headline than the one he began with. And he starts again. Be prepared for that.

Expect to start again.

The trial page is only a trailer for what is to come. It is a means of releasing thoughts rather than fashioning them in your best words. At this stage what is needed are thoughts pinned to the page in note form – and any order.

Do not attempt to impose an order.

If in doubt about the relevance of the thought – include it. Later the reverse of this rule will apply but right now you need every thought you can get your mind around. Your unconscious may be ahead of you. The relevance of the thought may not become apparent until hours later. It may connect with a subsequent thought.

Let your critical faculty relax. The more material the better. When you begin to structure your thoughts half of them may go. Even those you felt were essential. And an insignificant little item may assume importance. When you structure you make choices.

And the more items to choose from the better. So each thought must be a discrete whole. Separate it out. Give it a number.

I always use an old-fashioned exercise book. I list the thoughts on the right-hand page allowing the left for any comments or possible correction. Each thought is numbered and separated by one line from its neighbour.

One word of caution: at this stage do *not* subdivide. Do not number thoughts 2a, 2b, 2c, etc. It is too soon to make connections or impose an order. The sooner you impose an order the more restrictions you make upon your flow of material. Another danger in sub-numbering is that it may create a hierarchy – major thoughts and minor thoughts. It is too early to make value judgements. All thoughts are equal. Tomorrow is time enough for some to be more equal than others.

You may find it difficult to be this unselective and uncritical, particularly if you have to untrain a trained mind. In that case impose some unusual order upon your material. Set yourself a target of, say, thirty thoughts. Make quantity rather than quality (even relevance) your aim. Number odd lines on the page and fill them. Or try to think of an item to fit each letter of the alphabet.

The skills you need in assembly are precisely the opposite of those you will need when writing your presentation. Order, logic, single-mindedness...put them on the substitutes' bench. Not simply because a premature order will restrict flow but because *creativity feeds on disorder.*

You must regard the assembly of material – and a deeper subsequent writing – as a creative exercise. Ideas happen when thoughts collide. The poet's mind, according to T. S. Eliot, is 'constantly amalgamating disparate experience'.[1]

You must encourage collision. Not all collisions are productive. However, the more thoughts the more chances of collision. The more collision the greater chance of productive collision.

Your notes are not a record simply of what you already know. You must speed-read what others have written on the subject. Some of their arguments you may wish to use to reinforce your own, or constructively reject, replacing them with a new thought, i.e. a thought you did not have before opening the book. You are reading not for pleasure but for stimulus and increased awareness. Check the author's bibliography. Try to pursue the most interesting volumes.

Chase ideas no matter where they seem to lead.

And above all *read around* the subject. Look, for example, at the historical, social or industrial context. Do they order matters better abroad? Ask questions. Why? What? Who? What happened before? What will happen after? Spread yourself. Practise lateral thinking. If possible discuss your thoughts with other people. Brainstorm. Use their input. But remember the golden rule of brainstorming. No negatives. Someone suggests something impractical. Don't rubbish it, build on it. At this stage remember you must not be critical of others or yourself.

Follow Edward de Bono's advice and force yourself to make connections between the subject in hand and a word drawn at random from a dictionary.

And keep the subject in mind – consciously or probably unconsciously – whilst you engage in other activities. It's surprising how much extra material, seemingly extraneous, will become relevant.

Be uninhibited! Relax. Enjoy the freedom. If necessary have a drink and trust your unconscious – *it's on your side.*

Trust your unconscious

And if and when you get stuck and thoughts dry up do something else. Leave the project with your automatic pilot. Most studies of creativity – whether scientific discovery or artistic endeavour – reveal a common sequence: an initial period of conscious application followed by rest during which, however, the unconscious brain is busy connecting ideas which possibly the conscious brain might ignore or reject. Then the conscious brain takes over again and evaluates the suggestions. Scientists frequently affirm that their moments of insight happened away from the laboratory.

But serendipity has to be earned. You've got to know what you're not looking for. As Louis Pasteur put it, 'chance favours the prepared mind'. Serendipity thus is a bonus. But you will not benefit if you give it nothing to feed on.

But if note taking, reading in and around the subject and flying on automatic pilot stimulate insight, so above all does the act of writing itself. You write what you know and what you will know.

Writing is not mere transcribing. The vision, the idea, says C. E. Montague, 'comes into existence while the technical and physical work of writing goes on'. When you are actually *writing* 'the cold engine of the mind is warmed a little'.[2]

Do not wait until you have a perfect speech in your mind before beginning to write. And above all do not be fooled into thinking that all you need to do it is transcribe the perfect conception onto paper. It is neither as easy nor as straightforward as that. Writing will transform your concept. It will also inevitably transform your material.

'Milton only discovered that totality of what he meant by Lycidas in the act of writing it.'[3] You should know more about your subject and your relation to it when you have finished writing the speech than you did at the completion of your assembly.

Writing is a process not simply of putting together your well-ordered thoughts into a communicable form, but also of thinking new thoughts and accordingly of reordering your material. (And occasionally this process continues during the delivery of the speech itself!)

During writing you must expect to be surprised. You must be prepared to start again. You must keep your options open. Do not be seduced by the neat plan which is forming in your mind.

And be careful about the title. You may have to provide it before the speech is written – for advance publicity. Your title should play to your *purpose* and ideally your *point*. If you have not yet achieved your *point* make sure that it does not restrict you. Do not opt out by providing a bland title. Instead think of being provocative. You can always provide a subtitle on or near the day. And provided the title you originally gave plays to your *purpose* nobody will accuse you of irrelevance.

The title, or probably a *working* title, can act as a stimulus. It can generate a few trial pages. See where they lead and don't worry if you are surprised. Worry only if you are not surprised.

A working title is a useful catalyst. It may fulfil its entire function if it simply starts things moving. An enzyme's job is to cause a chemical reaction. This continues after the enzyme has said goodnight.

Writing a few trial pages will probably cause you to rethink your approach. A better shape may involve replacing the outline you have in mind. Some material is now seen as less relevant. New material may have to be sought. Do not fret. Do not regard the previous effort as wasted – but as a necessary preliminary. The assembly, the reading, the thinking, the conscious and unconscious making of connections, have helped you reach your point even if you have not yet articulated it. Without the effort you would not be where you are, i.e. ready to begin structuring.

Now is the time to distinguish the important thoughts from those less distinguished – maybe with asterisks; to list thoughts; to make groups; above all to cut, to edit.

And editing, as we shall see, is a process of illumination.

7   Patterns of Presentation

The key to a good presentation is structure – how it is put together. There are two aspects of structure:

(1) Structure of the presentation itself.
(2) Structure of the language.

The first concerns the grouping, shaping and ordering of the arguments. The second concerns the grouping, shaping and ordering of the sentences. This and the following three chapters deal with the former.

'All activity of an orator', says Cicero, 'falls into five divisions:

– hit upon what to say

– manage and marshal his discourses, not merely in orderly fashion but with a discriminating eye for the exact weight as it were of each argument

– array them in the ornaments of style

– keep them guarded in his memory

– deliver them with effect and charm'.[1]

We have reached Cicero's second part. We have hit upon what we want to say. The presentation structure, remember, is 'profoundly a result of its intention'. It has to fulfil your purpose. There is one, optimum, structure for achieving this. One.

Suppose your material consists of five key elements. There are therefore no fewer than twenty ways of arranging those elements. Not all of them will fail to fulfil your purpose. But only one sequence will fully achieve your intention.

Organization is the key to clarity.

It's time for order, logic and single-mindedness to leave the substitutes' bench.

We left your notes in Chapter 6 unnumbered and about to be organized. We now need to

(1) **evaluate**
(2) **eliminate**
(3) **group**

Go through your notes and mark each important item with, say, an asterisk. Put what you believe is your main thought (it would have earned two asterisks) in the middle of a sheet of paper. This thought should illustrate the point of your presentation.

Now begin to relate one thought to another. Re-read your notes and assemble them around the main thought. Items which are very close (i.e. subsets) should be grouped with the main thought in a box. Clusters of the other thoughts should similarly be grouped together in separate boxes.

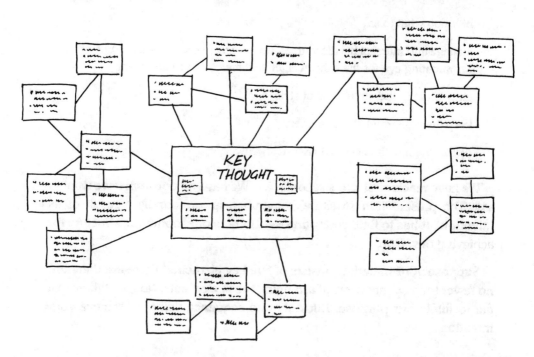

If all the thoughts don't fit into a box put them into a margin.

You will now have a central box of thoughts, other boxes of thoughts radiating from it plus a collection of unclassified thoughts. These 'thoughts' may in fact be nothing more than numbers – i.e. the original numbers you gave the notes you made.

At this stage you are working out relationships, patterns of thought. The separate boxes relate to the central box. The overall pattern is spatial. It has – as yet – no time sequence. The main box may represent the beginning of the speech. More likely it will represent the body of the speech. Other subsets will have to be made. A sequence may be apparent at this stage. What matters, however, is that a total argument is seen to emerge. How far does the complete picture radiate naturally from the central thought? Is the structure *coherent*?

Before you number the boxes in a time sequence you need to know if your form is organic. Coleridge described organic form as 'innate; it shapes as it develops itself from within, and the fullness of its development is one and the same with the section of the outward form'.[2]

If each of the boxes does not radiate naturally from the centre it will be difficult to make your speech coherent or even interesting. Unrelated items do not constitute a speech. Art is about relationships. So is science. 'Information, no matter how reliable or extensive, which consists of a set of isolated properties is not science.'[3]

The scheme is a result of the *purpose*. The centre of your pattern is the *point* you want to make over all others. And the 'all others' must radiate logically from that centre.

In *Phaedrus* Plato has Socrates criticize a poet's epitaph for the random order of his lines: 'any speech ought to have its own organic shape like a human being ... *it must have a middle and extremities so composed as to fit one another and the work as a whole*'.[4]

I hope by now that it is clear that there are two stages to structuring your presentation. They are a consequence of the media you are using. These are

(1) spatial.
(2) temporal.

The pattern on your sheet of paper is spatial. It will reveal whether you have an organic presentation. Creating a coherent design is the first step in ensuring that your audience receives what you intend. The next step is to transform the spatial design into a time sequence. It may be a question of simply numbering your boxes in your order of delivery. But, as before, be prepared to start again.

It is unlikely, for example, that your central box will become the introduction. The introduction will have to be carefully fashioned. It may reside in one of the other boxes or the margin or need to be thought out anew. The separate boxes may have to be rearranged, i.e. differently from the order of degree of relevance to the central box, let alone the order in which you devised them. More probably they will have to be unpacked and the contents reorganized.

Remember our two rules:

Think like the listener.
Write like a good talker.

Is it likely that the pattern on the page can be received in that form without assistance?

You must reshape the material to assist reception of your argument.

Perhaps you can better appreciate the difference between spatial and temporal patterning by imagining that you have been to an interesting presentation. A friend asks you 'what did he say?' You respond by giving the main argument, some of the contributory points. Your friend asks a second question. 'How did he say it?' 'Well', you say, 'it was very interesting. He began with a story. It took place in ancient Rome. Then he showed a slide of a cutting from last week's *New Scientist*...'

Spatial patterning concerns the *what*.

Temporal patterning concerns the *how*.

Temporal patterning is necessary also for the written piece, since the argument will be read *in* time. But it is far more important, obviously, in a presentation given the evanescence of the spoken word.

By this time then you have

• a purpose

- a point

- and an argument which hangs together.

How do you tell it?

The choice can stupefy you. The following check-list is not exhaustive. Clearly nowhere near all the examples are relevant for any individual presentation. Check-lists are no substitute for work but they can suggest new directions and, at worst, guard against accidental exclusion.

Types of presentation structure

Classical

This is the usual format – 'tell them what you're going to tell them; tell them; then tell them you've told them'. It is very simple and you should not scorn simplicity. Its problem is of course the structure of the middle section and the difficulty of maintaining interest. Having stated your conclusion in your introduction you may find it difficult to surprise the audience in the long period in between. The danger is that you repeat yourself, play everything on one note.

Questions

This is a variant on the classical but more involving for the audience. Instead of stating your conclusion you ask questions which will be answered by the time the conclusion is reached.

'I want to ask three questions. Where is this company going? How is it going to get there? And what will it cost?'

Theme and Variations

This variant of the classical answers the problem of the middle plateau. The introduction makes the key point. This is then examined from different perspectives.

For example, the subject is industrial marketing. The *purpose* of our presentation is to convince an audience of engineers that marketing is not a soft discipline. The *point* we wish to make is that the consequences of marketing are *tangible*.

Having stated the point we would then illustrate it by means of various examples (e.g. a consumer-packaged goods item, a service industry, a government authority) before homing in on some engineering examples. We would show instances of both successful and unsuccessful marketing. We might end with a success story the audience knows and surprise them by pointing out that the engineering breakthrough which the product represents would never have brought dividends if the customer had not been researched and the product positioned correctly against the customers' needs, etc., etc.

Note that the variations provide light and shade. And that the closing in from consumer groups to engineering products is a *temporal* structure.

The List

This is a common format and not to be encouraged, though there are occasions when a list is inevitable. Some lists have been memorable. Or rather the *titles* have been memorable. Woodrow Wilson's Fourteen Points. The Ten Commandments. You stand a better chance in single figures – Roosevelt's Four Freedoms, for example.

But the problem with all lists is that they are spatial rather than temporal. The random thoughts could be expressed in any order and with no effect on the sense.

1, 2, 3, etc. by themselves are not dramatic. Nor is the alphabet, despite the assertion that a certain well-known actor could declaim the London phone directory and make it exciting. Listing your notes in alphabetical order is an easy way out. The writer's only justification is that the reader can look up the subject he needs (always provided he knows it is included). There is no justification for the speaker. The alphabet does not aid comprehension.

One device marginally more acceptable is the acronym. A speech on 'Creativity and radio advertising' could list five characteristics of the medium: rapport with the listener; accessibility; definition; immediacy; one-to-one communication. At the end the speaker sums up and – surprise! –

the initial letters of the criteria spell 'Radio'. It is a corny trick but very effective.

Categories

These are similar to lists. The subject matter is broken down according to the standard classifications, e.g. geographical, social, age.

Again there is very little natural drama in this approach, but remember the audience and the end. If you are addressing the Croydon Rotary Club you will not begin with Croydon and end with Agadir.

Time – Past and Future

Can the material be arranged according to time? Can a story be told – starting at the beginning and finishing at the end? And if so, is that order relevant?

What if the perspective is changed and the speaker predicts what will happen? The future of course lacks the logic of the past. The present seems logical but the past has settled down. Hindsight has imposed an order we may not have recognized at the time. One way of imposing an order on the future is to view it from a vantage point some years hence. Describe the future by looking back on it.

Pro and Con

This is another common format. Students are taught to answer examination questions this way: 'Shakespeare was not of an age but for all time: discuss.' The evidence for and against is assembled under those headings. Then either each heading is discussed pro and con or all the pros are enumerated, followed by all the cons (or vice versa).

Then a balance is struck. The essayist comes to a just and impartial conclusion. The scales are possibly still moving.

There is some drama in the pro and con but there is usually little passion, and although it may suit the examination room does it really fit the intent of the *presenter*? He operates in a commercial context. His job is to *persuade*. He must put certain arguments, but he must counter them.

A more intellectual and dramatic variant is to move from thesis and antithesis to synthesis. The conflict of pro and con has produced a new entity. The argument has been resolved during the time of the presentation.

Problem Solution

This shares the previous format's dramatic quality. The problem is stated, various solutions are examined and rejected. Gradually the objections are resolved. Eventually the solution is put forward and all the objections are answered. The problem is resolved – during the time of the presentation.

Anarchic

Well handled, this approach can be a huge success. Items are presented in no apparent order. Since there is no temporal sequence to assist the listener, his attention has to be seduced by the manner of the presenter, the light and shade. The individual items are short, varied, transmitted in quick succession. The absence of structure is the presenter's *raison d'être*. The listener, if seduced, will try to work it out for himself.

At the end the presenter rearranges the pieces of the kaleidoscopic picture to reveal a pattern. It is an answer to an unspoken but implicit question.

The presentation works like a pointilliste painting, which can be understood only by standing back some five metres from the canvas.

End First

In some respects this is the reverse of the previous format. The presenter begins with his conclusion. Surprise is sacrificed but drama need not be. The question – particularly if the conclusion itself is provocative – is how on earth will the speaker get there? It is the equivalent of the alternative detective story format – not a whodunnit, but a how-did-he-do-it?

In Medias Res

Just as you have started at the end, so you can start 'in the middle of things'. This was the technique of epic poets who, knowing their audience, began by jumping into the action, then putting it into context.

The novelist adopts the same technique. The film scenario also – moving from a scene of action to a flashback of exposition.

Narrative

Narrative is the oldest oral format. The story-teller engages our interest by introducing us to a character with whom we can identify and involving him (and therefore us) in a situation or series of incidents which has us wondering what will happen next.

In narrative, description is secondary. The story is all. The message is not overt. It is rendered through the story.

But how can your subject be converted into narrative?

There is one simple way. You tell the story of preparing your speech.

'Six weeks ago if somebody had asked me to speak on X...' etc. Then plot your learning process, your discovery of key points. In preparing a speech there is always a moment of truth. As previous chapters have indicated, there are setbacks and new starts. It's a sort of 'presenter's progress' which could well hold the attention of your audience.

Drama

Of course every presentation should be dramatic. However, drama itself could provide a model for a presentation, particularly, given the limited time and specific purpose, the strict discipline of Greek tragedy. The so-called Aristotelian Unities are very relevant: action, time and place. The play should be single-minded, happen in the time it takes to stage, occur in one location. Substitute 'presentation' for 'play' in that sentence and you have a reliable formula for a tight presentation.

There must be conflict. This could be provided by alternative courses facing our hero, the presenter. The drama reaches a crisis. The presenter resolves the crisis.

Curtain

But we're not through with structure. In the following chapters we'll examine beginnings, middles and ends and, more especially, the means by which individual parts are put together.

8   Beginnings

The first few minutes are an opportunity. Grasp it. But don't abuse it. Now you have their attention for free. Very soon you will have to earn it. How you begin represents a major investment.

Begin, as ever, by considering the audience. How have *you* felt as a listener when a presentation starts?

Have you responded to the speaker? Has he made you sit up? Has he intrigued you, amused you, set you thinking? Or have you felt embarrassed, annoyed, indignant?

If so ask yourself why. The answer inevitably is that he has *not done his homework*. Or, having done it, chosen to ignore it or been unable to put it across.

Quintilian said 'in every subject there is something or other naturally first.' [1] So naturally we must begin with Quintilian. He declared the object of an introduction is to secure

*   **goodwill,**
*   **attention,** and
*   **the wish for further knowledge.**

Goodwill

Communication is two-way. *Communicare* means to share. You must establish a relationship. This is difficult if the tone of voice is false or stilted. The script must not lock you into non-colloquial utterances. You should be prepared for the late inclusion of an appropriate ad-lib. But guard against the cheap or dubious gag.

You are beginning a *dialogue*. You could risk a question. But the golden rule of feedback is that feedback in turn demands feedback. If the audience responds you must, in turn, respond.

But the real dialogue should already be in the script. You have written the speech, remember, with your listener, Eric, in the chair opposite.

You gain goodwill by demonstration rather than statement. If you have spent four weeks researching the subject, don't tell the audience that. Let your speech be evidence.

How would you as a listener react to these two beginnings?

'I should like to share with you the results of four months' intensive study into the pre-Roman history of this part of London.'

or

'You probably know that this building is near the site of a Bronze Age encampment?' (*pause*) 'Yes, they found charred remains fifty yards (*pointing*) from that fire exit.'

Do your homework, do *not* tell them you've done it. Let them tell you.

The introduction should convince the audience that you know your subject and that you are in control of your material. There should be evidence too that you have organized it.

You should also demonstrate an awareness of the audience's needs, composition and interests. And remember that the audience is different from all other audiences. The moment you let them feel otherwise, that you've given this same speech to a dozen other audiences, you have lost their proffered goodwill.

Attention

There are many devices to catch the audience's attention. Personally I prefer to leave the stage trick to the body of the talk when attention may begin to wane. Begin with a trick and the audience will expect them throughout your talk. The element of surprise is lost.

At this stage you gain their attention best by involving the audience. Get them to do something ('I do, I understand'). I once addressed a marketing seminar on the subject of creativity in television advertising. I began by welcoming the delegates as if they were the jury of a TV awards festival. I 'reminded' them of the rules. The lights were lowered, the commercials were screened, the lights were raised and the seminar continued. Towards the end of the seminar a colleague interrupted me. The score sheets had been 'lost'. We ran the commercials again and asked the audience to mark a second time. Had they changed their opinions regarding specific advertisements and if so why? Was it something I said?

A participation exercise need not be this elaborate. If you provide pads and pens then, for heaven's sake, make sure they are used.

You can gain attention by all manner of means. But you need to progress. You need to gain – and maintain – *interest.*

And what everyone is interested in above everything else is himself. If you think like a listener you will the better enlist his *co-operation.*

The wish for further knowledge

If an introduction is meant to establish a relationship then it's crucial both parties want it to continue.

Too many introductions are unconnected to what follows. A speaker goes through the formality of thanks, greetings, favourite all-purpose jokes and anecdotes, a quick preliminary note about the matter in hand and then ... becomes somebody else. The honeymoon is over.

The introduction must be connected to the speech. It is not a hermetically sealed component. It must entice the listener. It must give him an idea of where the speaker intends to take him and how long the journey will last.

As the previous chapter has shown there is no one 'correct' format. The beginning can reveal the ending or maybe provide a glimpse.

But what it *must* provide is a route map.

You and the audience must be pointing in the same direction. You want it to 'wish for further knowledge' on *your* subject. The danger of a jokey, unconnected introduction is that the audience, by the time the introduction is over, may not know what that subject is.

You have blown your opportunity. Your introduction has generated noise rather than sound. (There will be enough noise in the hall without bringing your own in the text.)

You may have gained goodwill and initial attention and established a dialogue but you and the audience would be speaking different languages – a fact which will become only too clear when you get into your presentation.

Opening Gambit

The subject ('*Tell 'em*')

Simply state the subject you are addressing – and get on with it. The shock value of this bald approach may win over the audience. You may choose to state the *purpose* of your presentation. Refrain from stating the *point*. This ruins the drama.

A Question

Ask a question which the presentation will answer. You *might* try a rhetorical question – only be prepared for a reply.

A Joke

But make sure it is relevant. If you can genuinely refer to it again in the body of your presentation so much the better.

A Surprise

Again, relevance is the key. There is certain to be one fact among all the data you have researched which surprised you. Statistics are a ready source of surprises. Make sure you relate them to the audience. Don't talk percentages. It's not 20 per cent of the population but one person in five. Don't mention large sums but paint a picture. Not 200,000 people but 'you could fill Wembley Stadium twice over'.

A True Story

Don't cheat. Don't adapt a well-known anecdote and use the name of the chairperson. Instead search for a story which illustrates your purpose, if possible your point. If necessary tell a personal anecdote concerned, for example, with preparing the talk.

A Quotation

Search a book of quotations and, provided your selective perception is functioning, you will find at least one apt quotation within fifteen minutes. Of course one source of good quotations is the presentation itself. Quote yourself. You can be pretty sure it's relevant and that you'll repeat it. With luck so will the audience.

The conclusion you may have reached, if only in the last example, is that you might consider writing your introduction *last*.

9   Middles

Audiences quite like beginnings but *adore* endings. It's the bit in between which gives the greatest problem for the presenter. This is where you keep the promise of your introduction, get your message across, develop your argument and *take the audience with you*.

The art of putting it together is precisely that – being able to take the audience with you every step of the way. The argument must be developed carefully. It has to lead logically to your conclusion, to the point you are making. This does *not* mean that the conclusion need be evident from the start or even at the half-way stage. Too overt an approach may turn off an audience. Surprise is a useful weapon.

No, logical development means:

(1)   each step must be related to the previous step; and
(2)   by the time the conclusion is reached, the 'inevitability' of the route of the argument must be accepted.

The destination may well differ from what the audience expected but having got there they should not rub their eyes in disbelief. They participated in the development of the argument.

The presenter must at all times in the speech effect a *double relationship*:

(1)   **Internal**: the elements of the speech must relate to each other.
(2)   **External**: the relationships are presented in such a way that the audience can relate to them.

This demands that you begin the body of your speech with what the listener *knows*. You must build upon common ground. You may start the speech proper with a provocative remark, even with your conclusion if it is likely to surprise or shock the audience. (It will then wonder how you are going to prove your point.) But you must never begin your argument with a premise the audience does not by and large accept.

I once began a speech by declaring that advertisers must needs go over people's heads. I began the *argument* by speaking of the importance of targeting, i.e. selecting that section of the public for whom the product is meant. Speaking to *those* people may well distance you from the rest of the public, etc., etc.

It is very important to distinguish between the *introduction* and the *start of the argument* – another reason, I feel, for delaying the writing of the former until you have finished the latter.

Your argument must proceed from the known to the unknown. Remember Antony Jay's intellectual judo – the sport of using your listener's beliefs to *win* your argument.

You need to develop your argument in terms of the listener's attitude and acceptance. It is unlikely, therefore, that the structure you prepared in *ordering* your thoughts will hold for the writing of your *script.*

That previous structure I said would ensure you that you had a coherent argument. You now need to rejig those elements. The pattern of boxes radiating from a central box will, at the very least, need to be reordered into a linear sequence. More probably you will need to break up and reassemble the pieces.

The starting point for the previous structure was the *key thought* (the central box) of your argument. The starting point of the script structure is the *first thought* you need to get across.

Consequently the boxes and their contents must be examined *from the listener's point of view.* What is known and unknown? Where is there likely to be disagreement? What will cause difficulties? Where is the starting point? What can come next? You may be lucky and simply regroup the existing boxes. You may need to take one of the formats suggested in Chapter 7.

But merely putting the elements into a sequence which will assist the listener's understanding of your argument is no guarantee by itself that he will follow you every step of the way.

Presenters use the evanescent medium of sound. Your script must somehow compensate for the absence of a printed text, chapter headings, subheads and above all the ability to turn back, check and re-read.

You need to signpost.

You may choose to do that at the start by giving the audience a map of the course. You don't have to give everything away by telling them something of the route you intend to take. (If you have a small audience the map can be displayed on a flip chart, e.g. numbered segments of your presentation are listed.)

The word signpost is apt. Signposts point in more than one direction. You need to tell the audience both where you are going and where you have been.

Summing up every so often reinforces the learning process. But make sure the summation is seen both as a conclusion of what has gone and as a beginning, or basis, of what is to follow. The interim summary is a link.

The problem solution format (p. 50) is a good example of reinforcement at work. The stage-by-stage review of each solution's advantages and disadvantages implicitly repeats the problem whilst the intractability of the problem is seen to reduce.

Reinforcement is not the same as repetition. It is not a case of 'telling them while you're telling them'. You are on a journey, not marking time. Each interim summary is moving you and your audience forward. Together.

As it happens, you are the only one who knows what is round the next corner or beyond the immediate hill. You should encourage the audience by assuring it of experiences to come.

Give them a trailer – 'coming soon'. A preliminary warning of pleasures or even of difficulties ahead will alert them.

Give them a trailer

The odd aside, pause, looking forward or back ... all serve to maintain the tension. Don't overdo them; otherwise they become an irritating mannerism and you lose the very thing you are trying to obtain. In my experience many speakers are so preoccupied in arriving at their destination they spend very little time pausing to look at the scenery, with the result they arrive at the destination alone.

At all times relate to the audience. What does Eric feel about that last paragraph? You could actually incorporate his questions into your text. 'That's all very well, but how does that apply to council houses?' You proceed to answer it. Dialogue.

Narrative can be introduced as a change of pace. You may, for example, be using a straightforward format (say questions, p. 47). You then change into narrative (p. 51). For example:

> I want to stop there for a moment. Let me tell you, when I got to this point in preparing the speech I thought I knew all the answers. After all *(here you recapitulate — and lean forward)*, but for one niggling thought *(here you introduce a new idea and lead of course into the interim summary you have just made)*.

These devices are introduced to enable the listener to follow and understand your argument – and to *want* to. There are other means of obtaining interest – use of film, tapes, illustrations, etc. Antony Jay refers to these as 'texture'.

'Since attention diminishes after the first ten minutes', says Jay, 'it is in that period, until it climbs again, that the greatest care must be devoted to texture variance and other devices to revive and maintain attention.'[1]

Remember the attention curve. It starts high, gradually slips and perks up towards the end. Two factors tell the audience the end is in sight. One is the clock. The other is you. Signal the end but play fair. Don't say 'finally', and three minutes later 'in conclusion'.

Incidentally, if you get a dramatic response upon the word 'finally' (heads suddenly raised, pens put away, smiles all round) don't worry. It's too late to worry.

You may have followed all the preceding advice, taken the listener with you every step of the way. But the journey may quite simply have taken longer than it needed.

Finally...

AHA! That made you
sit up and take
notice, didn't it!

Do not attempt to fill the time you have been given. Start by cutting 15 per cent off the time to allow for natural expansion during the performance. Then see if you can write it to be spoken in five minutes less than that.

For example, you have allowed thirty minutes. 15 per cent equals four and a half minutes. Twenty-five and a half minutes minus five equals twenty and a half minutes. That's your target.

Our old friend Quintilian advised his orators to be

clear,
brief, and
credible.

Better cut now rather than at rehearsal let alone *during the speech* (which may be impossible if you are locked in to a slide sequence or out of contact with the crew).

You will need to be ruthless. You probably won't be able to say everything you would like to say. Nor everything you may feel the audience ought to know. Just make sure you say everything you need to say. That way your cutting will actually improve your structure. So there is a double advantage: the listener is both less likely to be bored and more aware of your argument.

'The secret of being a bore', said Voltaire, 'is to tell everything.' (*Sept discours en vers sur l'homme.*)

10 Endings

One advantage of not writing your introduction until you have reached the end is that you can make the two relate to each other. Be very careful, however, not to make them identical. This can happen if you follow the old 'tell them what you're going to tell them' approach.

Your introduction and conclusion should not be a pair of aural bookends.

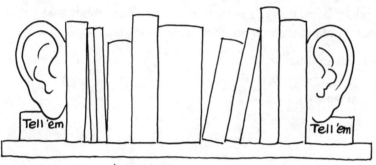

Aural bookends

That is not to say that they can't use the same or similar material. The way the material is *used* must be different. For example, you could repeat the introductory joke with a new twist. You could repeat the introductory quotation – but extend it. It is vital that the argument has developed. Merely putting the listener back where he started could convey the idea that you have wasted his time.

I am generally out of sympathy with the neat ending. Symmetry worries me. It sounds too much like the place where good ideas get buried.

Television and film people refer to the ending as the 'wrap up'. The last thing you want your listener to do is to regard your presentation as all packed up ready to be put away or sent somewhere. In fact the *last* thing you want your listener to do is wonder how you began this whole business. Remember? It's called the target response. What do you want the listener to think, believe, feel, do as a result of the presentation?

You need to leave your listener with a positive *reaction* to what you have said – followed by some appropriate *action*.

It is very tempting to 'wrap up', to say goodbye to our subject as well as our audience. It appeals to the craftsman in us.

We like to achieve perfection. But the object we are crafting here is not an end in itself. It is a means to an end. We are not inviting the audience to say 'amen'. We might hope they say 'great speech'. We would prefer them to say 'great idea' or 'you've made me think'. The greatest reaction I ever got was about six months after one presentation when I ran into a managing director who said he had restructured his company as a result!

Part of putting it together is *pulling* it together. But don't tie the thread into a pretty bow. Forget the yellow ribbon. Remember that yellow note. That post-it note you stuck on your desk. Your *purpose*.

So – to recap thus far ...

Don't just repeat.

Don't make it too neat.

Look backwards – while
pushing your audience
forward

There is thus an intriguing paradox about the conclusion of the presentation. You need to look backwards whilst at the same time pushing your audience forward – into some sort of action.

You need to reiterate various points and refresh their memory. You need to bring the presentation to a climax. You have after all to *sound* as though you're finishing – if only to alert the organizers or the tea lady.

But at the same time you want the audience to be moved towards action.

As you write your last sentence, what is Eric saying? 'So what?', or 'I knew all that – you've said it already'? If so you have merely succeeded in wrapping up. You *want* him to say something like 'You're right. I'll do something about it.'

So how to resolve this paradox? The temptation, of course, is to say something new. Avoid it. If that idea relates to your argument it should already have been included. If it does not – what on earth is it doing here? Particularly at the most important part of your presentation.

The conclusion is as big an opportunity as your introduction. Probably bigger – since people seem to remember longest the last thing they hear.

But if you can't say something new at least you can find a new way of saying something. By which I do not mean simple paraphrase. To paraphrase is to tread water. Your conclusion must move you (and your listener) forward.

There are at least three techniques to assist you.

1   Make the sum more than the parts

Repeat the points but give them an extra dimension. The simplest device is to pull them together with a mnemonic (see 'radio' on p. 48) or a rhyme or even a quotation. Sometimes the mere fact of laying bare your essential thoughts, side by side, will of itself produce a transmutation which you did not previously recognize.

Quintilian tells his orators to 'bring the whole subject under view at once and produce a cumulative effect through arguments which, taken separately, had less weight.'[1] Synergy, in other words, can't happen until the individual parts are brought together.

Market summary
National requirements
Economic forecast
Motivation
Overseas trade
New dispensation
Implementation
Conclusion

2   Change your style

The conclusion is an opportunity not only to build on what has preceded but also to capitalize on the relationship you have (with luck and good judgement) effected. You need at this stage to change your approach entirely. After all the audience should by this time feel it knows you. If you have made your point they may be expecting you to 'ask for the order'. If you are to end with an injunction then you will certainly have to appeal to both reason and emotion.

A lucid presentation can afford to end on a passionate note – provided of course that the passion is seen as relevant to the argument.

But passion is only partly in the performance. Eloquence demands the appropriate language. Purple patches should be struck from the body of your script. But at the end?

Here's Quintilian again. In the conclusion (peroration) he writes 'we are free to open the floodgates of eloquence. If we have treated the rest successfully we shall now hold the attention of our hearers and we may employ language and sentiments characterized by magnificence and beauty.'[2]

A new way of saying something may make that something more deeply felt. In the body of your script it is prose. Here it is in a sense poetry. The difference between the one and the other lies in the intensification with which a subject is viewed. The poet looks at the familiar and sees it anew –

and is able to communicate that intensity of vision to a third party. Suddenly the importance, relevance, significance to the listener of what he has already heard becomes more acute.

3   Sharpen your point

We have already touched on this in Chapter 5 where we discussed purpose and point. Then it was suggested that the presenter could sum up his key argument in a slogan.

Do this if at all possible. And avoid pre-empting it during the body of your presentation. In other words your point can be expressed throughout the presentation in plain speech. The slogan takes the argument that one, essential, insightful step further at the very end.

I recently gave a presentation on the subject of creativity in radio commercials. My purpose was to urge the young audience to start with the product and work outwards. Not vice versa. Not to imitate existing forms of radio commercials or use material from other sources such as radio or television programmes or popular culture – what is known in the trade as 'borrowed interest'.

Early on in the talk I quoted Leo Burnett who said that there is drama in every product, and that the copywriter's job is to dig for it.

When I reached the conclusion I re-read the text. And the Burnett quotation enabled me to sharpen the point.

'There is still plenty of drama beneath the surface of products. Interest does not have to be borrowed – but burrowed.'[3]

Finally (your cue to sit up) what about concluding with a joke?

I devote a chapter later to the subject of humour. As you will see I am greatly in favour – provided it is relevant. The danger of a joke at the end of a presentation is that the laugh may deflect the audience from your purpose. Relevant jokes are thin on the ground. You can of course force some sort of connection with your subject but it is very difficult to find a joke which illustrates your *point*.

Ask yourself why you need a joke at the end. 'Always leave 'em laughing' may be good practice for an entertainer but if your purpose is to communicate and inspire action then how does that laugh help you? The introductory joke may well help you establish rapport but the time for that is now well past!

But if you can sum up your point with a witticism – in other words a slogan which is also amusing – then you may hit upon the best of all conclusions.

For example, you are speaking on the subject of dangerous driving. The point is that ultimately the only problem the listener can do something about is his own capability at the wheel. 'Safety begins at home.' 'Safety is in your own hands', perhaps. But the audience would be more likely to remember *this* summation:

'The car to watch is the car behind the car in front of you.'

11   Structuring the Language

We turn now from the structure of the components of the speech to the structure of the language. From the thoughts to the words used to express those thoughts.

The purpose of the presentation is to pass a thought from one mind to another – and to get the receiver to act in the way intended. Language is the means by which the thought is both formed and expressed. The more clearly formed in the sender's mind, the more clearly expressed and the more efficient the transmission.

The test of efficiency is comprehension. This of course applies equally to the written and to the spoken text. (The latter is easier to verify by means of feedback.) Indeed most of the principles of good written prose apply to presentation language. The means of achieving them, however, are different.

This chapter deals with the general principles of good prose. The following chapter examines the nature of the differences (which are caused by the demands of the listener and the evanescent nature of sound). Thereafter we examine the tools of language, imagery, style and rhythm – and how the presenter should use them.

The purpose of language is to get our thoughts across. This means

(1)   our words must mean to the receiver what they mean to us;
(2)   they must be put together in a manner which does not alter the meaning.

Our choice of words (1) and our choice of structure (2) are both critical. In English these choices are very wide.

We are blessed with synonyms and words differing in subtle nuances. Our verbs have different tenses and moods. Choose wrongly and our early lucidity disappears in the writing. How often have you said 'I *know* what I want to say, but I just can't seem to write it'?

Then, having written it to our satisfaction, we may have communicated something unintended or confusing to the receiver.

Comprehension is the test. At all times you must ask yourself 'is this what I mean?' and ask Eric 'what does it mean to you?' If something is not clear re-read the text and check for *sharpness*.

(1)   Are any words or terms *ambiguous*?
(2)   Is the subject of each sentence absolutely clear?
(3)   Are the words, sentences, allusions:

> general instead of *specific*?
> vague instead of *definite*?
> abstract instead of *concrete*?

(4)   Are your verbs passive instead of *active*?

Specific, definite, concrete, active – all sharp words. Your language must be lucid, clear, forceful – particularly if you are using it to get something done.

Check next for *length*.

(5)   Would the sense be improved with fewer words?
(6)   With shorter words?
(7)   With shorter sentences?

For the presenter language is a set of tools. Examine what you have written. Do you feel you can *handle* those thoughts, pick them up? If not, neither can the audience.

What are you trying to say? Are these the best words with which to express it? Are they in their best order?

If you are still unhappy go back.

(8)   Do you really know what you want to say?

If the language isn't right the thought isn't right. 'If language is incorrect', says Confucius, 'then what is said is not meant. If what is said is not meant then what ought to be done remains undone.'

Language acts upon thoughts as litmus paper upon acidity. It reveals unclear thinking. As Orwell said, sloppy language is a result of sloppy thought. If we can't express it maybe there was no 'it' in the first place. If we fudge and try to disguise our inadequate thought in a coating of words, we create an imprecise language which in turn encourages further imprecise thoughts.

The opposite of sharp is blunt. Language must be a precise tool, not a blunt instrument. The opposite of sharp is also unfocused. Presenters seem to worry more about focusing their pictures than their words.

Prose, said Orwell, often 'consists less and less of words chosen for their meaning and more and more of phrases tacked together like the sections of a prefabricated hen-house'.[1]

(9) Are parts of your text 'ready-made'?

Ready-made phrases may seduce the listener with their familiarity, which may suggest a certain authority. This probably false and, at best, borrowed authority may also fool *you* into believing you have said something important.

Clichés are ready-made. They save mental effort.

Clichés are unfocused. The original image is blurred to the point of invisibility. If I mention a 'sea of faces' you register a crowd, a lot of people. Do you actually see a moving mass of people swaying in *waves*, as a crowd at a cup final? I doubt it.

Avoiding hackneyed, meaningless phrases... is what speech making is all about

Usage has blurred the sharpness. And almost certainly the context in which the phrase was first used is not your context. But if it fits your context *and any context* what point is there in using it?

Not only do the clichés save *your* mental effort, they save the listener's. He is not kept busy. Clichés don't involve, they reassure. It's a familiar landscape where every row is hard to hoe, each lily is gilded, each mule is stubborn, oxen are strong and hay is made while the sun shines. He's heard it all before. Do you really want your listener to say *that* at your presentation?

Answering our final question may solve many of the problems of a difficult text.

(10)   What happens if you try to change every word?

Can you do it, and maintain your meaning? Or – dare we suggest it? – does the use of different words make the meaning clearer? Are you left with more words or fewer? Are there words which are absolutely irreplaceable?

And which version does Eric prefer?

12   The Language of Speech

The purpose of spoken language is no different from that of written language. And as before, this means:

(1)   our words must mean to the receiver what they mean to us;
(2)   they must be put together in a manner which does not alter the meaning.

Achieving these ends is more difficult with the spoken than with the written text – particularly for the literate person.

Speaking we regard as 'natural'. The rules of oral grammar, according to Ong, 'live in the unconscious in the sense that you know how to use the rules and even how to set up new rules without being able to state what they are.'[1]

But colloquial speech is regarded by literate people as inferior. Witness what happens when natural speakers pick up the pen. They adopt a new role, 'put on their best clothes'.

Writing somehow demands a formality which would be found 'unnatural' in conversation, indeed a hindrance. Yet capturing the informality of colloquial speech in the written text is a task either beyond most people or regarded by some as unworthy. The two languages are divided by a 'class barrier'. The literary is posher than the oral. Only the élite can write. There are three thousand spoken languages of which only seventy-eight have a literature.[2] Presenters are literate. That's half the trouble.

It's very difficult for the literate presenter to imagine a language without texts. Without reading and writing how could he recall his thoughts? What techniques would he adopt? Might he try some form of memory training? Might not that memory training exist within the spoken text itself? Words and phrases would be repeated. Rhythm and even rhyme could help register the thoughts. He would be like a ballad maker, repeating key lines and choruses.

The pattern would be crucial – and in no way the same as that of the written text. The ephemeral has to be altered to make it hang on.

Speech is basic and primary. It has a 'functional priority. "Spoken language" serves in a wider range of communicative functions than does written language.'[3] Utterances can become permanent by being transferred to written form. Sounds become graphic shapes, and these are easier to examine, rearrange. You can relate them to each other (syntax) and to things (semantics). Spoken words are very different from written words. The first are structured in time. The second are structured in space. You can see what you are doing once your thoughts are visualized on the page. You can subordinate one to another. Oral cultures are 'additive rather than subordinative', says Ong.[4] In other words a speaker is more likely to add one thought to another with 'and' rather than subordinate one to another with 'which'. He will say

(a) I went to the match last Saturday. Half-time there was a demonstration.

He will *not* say

(b) During half-time at last Saturday's match there was a demonstration.

(a) is two sentences, though in fact three equal discrete elements (match/half-time/demonstration). (b) is one sentence with one major element (demonstration) and two minor, subordinate elements (match/half-time).

The absence of a written text means the absence of a 'backloop'. Putting across an argument in a purely spoken text demands that both the sender and the receiver are simultaneously at the same place in the argument. In a written text if the author is ahead of the reader, the reader can pause (and automatically the author does too), whilst he goes back (with the author) to a previous part of the track. The presenter has to fashion his text to ensure *simultaneous comprehension*.

Breaking up the thought into separate elements is one way of ensuring this.

You can prove it for yourself. Here is a piece of written text:

The bicycle next to the green car in the car-park belongs to the housekeeper's brother-in-law.

Suppose you wish to communicate that thought to a colleague. How would you do it? Would you speak the above sentence? Very unlikely.

Just imagine you are standing by a window overlooking the car-park ... what would you say? How many sentences would you use? Where would you *begin*? You would say something like this:

'See the car in the car-park? The green one? See the bike next to it? Well, you know the housekeeper? That bike belongs to her brother-in-law.'

What has happened?

1   More sentences

We have broken up the text. Instead of one sentence – five. Instead of one compact, multiple element sentence, a sequence of sentences each containing one discrete element.

Oral culture is additive rather than subordinative. Spoken English moves in a simple straight line – a sequence of short sentences. Full stops separate them. They are joined by 'ands' and 'buts', rarely by relatives such as 'who' and 'which'.

2   More words

We have used more words. Not fifteen but twenty-six. A 40 per cent increase. But what do we notice about those extra words? They do *not* represent new thoughts.

3   Redundancy

We have repeated ourselves. The traditional term for this is **redundancy**.

Redundancy is the repetition of words and phrases which, though strictly speaking unnecessary to the meaning, are probably necessary for the understanding.

Such redundancy on the page would be an overkill of information. It may be redundant to say 'A-apple' when either 'A' or 'apple' will do logically. But redundancy aids accurate decoding – and helps to overcome noise on the channel. The extra words may not represent extra information and therefore could be regarded as inefficient. But since, by reinforcing existing information they help transmission, they are in reality very efficient.

The presenter who uses redundancy is conscious of the listener's needs. He is bringing the listener along every step of the way. Simultaneous comprehension. The presenter must be careful that he doesn't overdo it. The more he researches the audience the more he learns about their knowledge of the subject. The more they know the less redundancy he needs to supply. Similarly, the more intellectual they are the better their ability to hold one part of a sentence in suspension before arriving at the conclusion and making the connection. But this does not permit you to present your material in any order (see point 5, p. 77).

Popular oratory contains more redundancy than a lecture to an intellectual gathering.

How much of this 1940 speech by Winston Churchill is necessary to understanding?

> We shall not flag or fail. We shall fight in France, we shall fight on the seas and the oceans, we shall fight with growing confidence and growing strength in the air, we shall defend our island, whatever the cost may be, we shall fight on the beaches, we shall fight on the landing grounds, we shall fight in the fields and in the streets, we shall fight in the hills; we shall never surrender.

Delete the repetition. Not only do you diminish the power but you reduce the chance of understanding. Redundancy keeps the listener with you. Substitute a comma for each 'we shall fight' (e.g. 'shall fight in France, on the seas and oceans ... on beaches, landing grounds, fields') and the listener might not keep up.

Remove redundancy from speech and you dispense with 'hello', 'please' and 'thank you'. They may add little information but they do communicate respect for, and interest in, the receiver which may in turn aid the successful reception of the information. Which brings us to the fourth change we effected to the 'car-park' text.

4   New form

We have turned the text into one half of a dialogue. Of the five sentences, no fewer than four are questions. We may not stop long for an answer but the listener has the opportunity to stop us if we can't answer him (silently to himself).

Our fifth and final change is the most important.

5   New order

We have ordered the elements for comprehension. The order is:

car-park
green car
bike
housekeeper
brother-in-law

We have taken the receiver from the known to the unknown. Each element is built upon what has gone before. This is what the film editor does. A film consists of separate shots. The sequence of the shots suggests relationships. The relationships create the meaning. The syntax of film is very like the syntax of speech. And vice versa. In our example, the first sentence ('See the car in the car-park?') is a long shot. We close into a medium shot ('The green one?') before panning to the bicycle ('See the bike next to it?'). Then we cut to a close-up ('Well, you know the housekeeper?') before pulling out to a two-shot ('That bike belongs to her brother-in-law').

Each sentence is a single thought and though there may be an infinite number of ways of arranging those sentences there is *only one best order* for comprehension.

We seem to understand the order instinctively when we engage in conversation but we lose the knack when we start to write spoken text.

That's where our friend opposite is so useful. We must arrange the sentences in such a way that we 'get the nod'. We start with the known and move step by step to the unknown. We go from agreement to disagreement; from the general to the particular; from the present to the future.

And with each sentence is a connecting point – a link word which joins up with a word or group of words in the immediately following sentence or refers back to a word or group of words in the immediately preceding (or recent) sentence.

Here is a crude example – an imaginary radio commercial from the USA of the Thirties:

(1)   And now a message from our sponsor, Flako.
(2)   Flako.
(3)   Flako Flour makes the flakiest pastry.

(4)   If you want pastry that really flakes you need flour that's really fine.
(5)   And folks that means Flako.
(6)   Flako the flakiest flour.
(7)   So ask for Flako.
(8)   And remember folks ... Flako spelt backward is OK ALF.

Let us look at the links. 'Sponsor' (1) is linked to Flako (2). Sentence (3) refers back and moves forward with two words, 'flakiest pastry', which link 'pastry' and 'flakes' (4). 'Flour that's really fine' (4) links with 'that' (5), etc., etc.

Somewhat less obvious is the structure of the accomplished orator. Here is the beginning of Victor Hugo's tribute on the centenary of Voltaire's death.

A hundred years ago today a man died. He died immortal. He departed laden with years, laden with the most illustrious and fearful of responsibilities, the responsibility of the human conscience informed and rectified. He went cursed and blessed, cursed by the past, blessed by the future; and these are the two superb forms of glory.

That is an orator's speech. The structure helps the audience comprehend – and the orator remember.

Analyse Hamlet's 'to be or not to be' soliloquy and you will find similar techniques; repetition of key words and the use of antithesis.

Is the reason actors find Shakespeare easier to memorise than modern dramatists the fact the Bard knew how to put it together?

13 The Language Toolkit

We'll now consider the tools of language – sentences, nouns, verbs, adjectives – and the means of arranging the constituents of the sentence, i.e. *syntax*.

The sentence

Each sentence is a binary unit. It consist of a **subject** and a **predicate** – the two parts of a proposition. Joining the two parts is a **copula** (e.g. the verb 'is').

The life of man (*subject*) is (*copula*) nasty, brutish and short (*predicate*).

The subject is the item you wish to talk about. And the predicate is what you have to say about it. If a sentence seems not to make sense, then, says Simeon Potter, it is because the writer has failed to keep those two things clear in his mind. He recommends asking yourself 'What is my *subject*? What do I *predicate* of that subject?' [1]

There are five — and only five — relationships between the subject and the predicate.[2]

EXISTENCE = S is P
CO-EXISTENCE = S and P both are
SEQUENCE = S precedes P
CAUSATION = S brings about P
RESEMBLANCE = S is like P

There are similarly only five types of sentence.[3]

statement
question
exclamation
wish
command

The presenter can maintain interest by departing from the most common form (i.e. the statement). Examine your script and count the non-statements. We've already recommended the occasional question (rhetorical or direct to the audience). Exclamations you should leave to the day (they should be genuine and therefore spontaneous), and 'military' commands should be left to the end. Ordinary commands (or requests) could occur frequently as you invite the audience to participate. And the odd wish can vary the texture of the speech – moving from direct speech to an aside. 'If only ...'

Finally there are only three ways of classifying sentences by *style*:

- *Loose* – facts listed one after another. This, you will notice, is very much as people talk, aggregative rather than analytic.
- *Periodic* – there is a climax at the end.
- *Balanced* – a balanced sentence, says Potter, 'may express two similar thoughts in *parallelism* or two opposing ones in *antithesis*'.[4]

The purpose of this analysis of sentences – by relationship of subject and predicate; by sentence type; and by style – is to remind the presenter of the choice at his disposal. Variety maintains interest.

You should also vary your sentence length. Sentences should average about twelve words. The majority should be short and crisp. Nevertheless a succession of short crisp sentences can become tedious. Similarly a succession of long ones can prove too demanding.

So can a sentence where the subject, verb and object are not close together. Suspended sentences are self-inflicted noise.

Syntax

Syntax means 'a connected order of things', or 'arranging together'. **PIT** is all about syntax. So, as we saw, is film editing. Shots are put together to make meaning; sentences likewise.

A text (written or spoken) is not just a sequence of sentences in any order. Each sentence has to relate to what has preceded it.

'It should always be clear', say Graves and Hodge, 'whether a sentence explains, amplifies or limits the statement it follows; or whether it introduces a new subject or a new heading of the original subject.'[5]

The statement is more important than any qualification. Make sure that the statement is clearly seen (and heard) for what it is. Give it a sentence to itself. Put any qualification in a subsequent sentence.

The analogy with film editing, and earlier with theatre, would seem appropriate for scripting a presentation. Actually 'drama is the key to all effective writing', say Fairfax and Moat, in their excellent popular primer '*The Way to Write*'.[6] A premise you can prove by reordering the parts of a sentence of a master author or poet. The order of the printed text gives the emphasis. The emphasis, they say, provides the drama.

The noun

A noun, we all know, is the name of a person or place or thing. It stands alone. In a sentence a noun can be the subject or the object.

But in another sense one sort of noun is always an object. Something you can pick up and feel. At least it should be – it's a **concrete** noun. Concrete nouns refer to things you *can* feel and/or see and/or touch and/or taste.

But **abstract** nouns refer to ... abstractions. You can't jingle them in your pocket or throw them at people or snuggle up to them. Death, eternity and the short span of life are concepts and difficult to get your mind round. Yet Andrew Marvell's couplet makes you see as well as think:

The grave's a fine and private place
But none, I think, do there embrace.

King Lear is a play about ingratitude. The old man is out in a storm. His daughters refuse him shelter:

> Mine enemy's dog,
> Though he had bit me, should have stood that night
> Against the fire.

Should you doubt the need to cram your presentation with concrete rather than abstract nouns ask yourself what you were thinking about earlier today. Or ask a listener what he remembers about a speech.

The verb

A verb is a doing word. Well ... yes. It can express action but it also expresses *being*.

There are two types – **transitive** and **intransitive**. Transitive means you do something to something else. Intransitive means you do something. For example:

'I told a joke.' (*transitive*)
'The audience was laughing.' (*intransitive*)

Words ending in '-ing' are called gerunds (Worthing, of course, is an exception.) They express a state. They are less active than the verb used in its simple present or simple past. Rather than 'the audience was laughing', 'the audience laughed'. Though not transitive, that is more *active*.

Wherever possible, use simple verbs in simple forms.

Which of these forms is the most dramatic?

'He examined the evidence. It proved that ...'
'Examining the evidence, he was able to prove that ...'
'The examination of the evidence proved that ...'

Try not to turn verbs into nouns. The nouns you create will be abstract. Besides, verbs move. Nouns don't. On the other hand – and for that reason – once in a while turn a noun into a verb. ('The labour we delight in physics pain.')

Your language must be dramatic. The basic sentence is

- **noun** (the doer)
- **verb** (the doing)
- **object** (the done to).

'The great strength of our language', says Ernest Fenollosa, 'lies in its splendid array of transitive verbs, drawn both from Anglo-Saxon and from Latin sources. These give us the most individual characterisations of force ... we do not say in English that things seem or appear, or eventuate, or even that they are; but that they *do*. Will is the foundation of our speech.'[7]

We do not say that things *are* ...? Right. Try to avoid the verb 'to be' and you'll be surprised what takes its place. Maybe nothing. Maybe the verb doesn't need to be there in the first place? Maybe the pace quickens ...?

Another accelerator is the *active* mood. Here the subject is the doer. Whereas in the passive mood the subject gets done. Which is more dramatic – 'Lineker hits the post', or 'The post is hit by Lineker'?

Make *your* subject the doer.

Change of tense can help speed the action. Most of the time, three will suffice: past, present and future.

Presentations are *live*. They demand the present tense. Occasionally we use future for effect. Often you need the past (e.g. narrative). When you mention an authority always use the present (even if, like Cicero, he has been dead a bit).

Conjunctions

Conjunctions are 'joining' words. They are natural in colloquial speech: 'And I said ...', 'And then the policeman took out his book...', 'And what do you think happened then?'

Conjunctions feature in loose sentences (lists of facts). Commas replace them in written text. They are often more effective than conjunctions in speech. A succession of short sentences standing alone may be better still. The 'ands' slow down the delivery, reduce the impetus of the script.

Longinus says 'If you tie runners together you will deprive them of their speed; in exactly the same way emotion resents being hampered by

If you tie runners together you will deprive them of their speed

conjunctions ... for it then loses its freedom of volition and the impression it gives of being shot from a catapult.'[8]

The adjective (and other modifiers)

The adjective is a describing word. But in describing it also qualifies. Sometimes this helps. Precision may assist you and the audience to focus. The adjective may provide essential information.

But check each one. Does it strengthen or weaken the noun? Voltaire was in no doubt. 'The adjective is the enemy of the noun.'

When Eliot writes:

The winter evening settles down
With smell of steaks in passageways[9]

do we need to be told it's a cold winter, that the steaks are frying? We know that.

Be sparing with your adjectives. One American schoolteacher asks her class to write a page of descriptive prose without using an adjective. Then they read what they have written and are allowed one adjective to place where they like – a golden coin to spend.

The adjectival phrase – a description of a few words – may or may not be necessary. Again check it out. Does it add? For example, in the following:

The tea, which had been standing half an hour, was cold.

The adverb qualifies the verb. 'Insults it', say Fairfax and Moat. 'The policeman ran quickly across the road.' (The adverb adds nothing.) 'Sweet Thames! run softly, till I end my song.' (Here the adverb surprises.)

The adverbial phrase also qualifies the verb. Too often the qualification is a cliché (with bated breath, with sinking heart, through thick and thin).

Qualifying phrases (adjectival or adverbial) hold up the progress of the argument. The pause must be worth it.

Franklin D. Roosevelt, 'For a Declaration of War against Japan', 8 December 1941:

Yesterday, December 7, 1941 – a date which will live in infamy – the United States of America was suddenly and deliberately attacked by naval and air forces of the Empire of Japan.

(A rare example of a successful modifier.) Remove modifiers and you put life back in your prose. Fairly, nearly, rather, little, pretty, somewhat, etc. have been called 'the leeches that infest the pond of prose, sucking the blood of words'.

And that – apart from prepositions, pronouns and interjections – is your complete toolkit.

14 Imagery

Imagery is an appeal to the senses. The writer uses word-pictures to illustrate, illuminate and embellish his thought.

An image, contrary to popular belief, is real. Which of the two following words provides a picture you can *see* – flamboyance or Liberace?

Imagery clarifies. It focuses, emphasizes. Its job is not to decorate but to assist the purpose of the writer.

Its basis is comparison. A **simile** is a likeness. One thing is said to resemble another. ('My love is like a red red rose.')

A **metaphor** replaces one thing with another. ('Our doubts are traitors.')

Imagery must be judged by its exactness. How apt is the image? Does it fit? More to the point, does it aid understanding and take meaning a step further? Poetry makes meaning more meaningful. A simile should illuminate. It should make the listener see better.

Poetry through impressions appeals to the imagination. Prose appeals to the reason. The first goes by way of the senses. The second by way of the intellect. That is the accepted wisdom. True. Except that reason and imagination trespass on each other's territory. Just as science makes common cause with art. 'Imagination is more important than knowledge', said Einstein (in his lecture 'Speaking of Science').

The image may move the argument forward more cogently than pure reason.

The allusion, analogy, simile, metaphor may more exactly express our thought than bald prose. The reaction we seek in our listener is both surprise and familiarity. A paradox? Yes. But we have all experienced this. Not the surprise which shouts 'Incredible!' but the surprise we feel when something is so right it clicks. The two elements fit into place. 'Freckles, like rust spots' says Willa Cather. We know what she is describing. We've seen them. The surprise we feel is the 'shock of recognition'. We have experienced this but never quite got the words together to say it. Irritating, isn't it! 'An irritable man is like a hedgehog rolled up the wrong way, tormenting himself with his own prickles.' I wish I'd said that. Alas, Thomas Hood got there first.

Shock of *recognition*. The comparison must not be far-fetched if it is to work. Nor too familiar either. We have to invent tomorrow's clichés.

But if simile is a conceit which we delight in, metaphor is no mere ornament but a pair of overalls we don in order the better to work out our thoughts. A metaphor extends our language. We transfer our thought processes from one set of words to another. The new terminology may provide new insight.

Whilst we lose ourselves in the terminology of the image, we still hang on to the object being compared. But, whereas a simile presents two pictures side by side, metaphor presents a single image viewed through bifocals.

'Metaphor', says Sir Herbert Read, 'is the expression of a complex idea, not by analysis or by direct statement, but by sudden perception of an objective relation.' [1]

See if this metaphor brings about a 'sudden perception'.

Imagine a man trying to console someone inconsolable. He says 'Time heals all wounds.' How would you describe his action? Here's how Shakespeare describes it – 'patch grief with proverbs'. (*Much Ado about Nothing* v, i, 17)

Exact. Compact. 'Poetry says more and in fewer words than prose' (Voltaire). But note that word 'patch' extends the meaning. Consoling and patching. This is more than the ability to see similarity in dissimilar objects. If simile adds then metaphor multiplies.

Provided it is fresh. Otherwise it will not be noticed.

Provided it is apt. Otherwise the meaning beyond meaning will not be seen.

And provided it is whole, unmixed.

15 Style

Ask a friend to imitate a public speaker and how would he begin? Possibly he would adopt a pose, put his hands on his lapels, peer over his glasses, and utter platitudes. Public speaking style.

This chapter is about style. *Your* style.

Is style necessary? Isn't clarity enough – the use of the right words in the right order? Intelligibility? Comprehension? If you can get a clear message out of your mind into that of the listener . . . what do you need with style?

'Good writers', says Ezra Pound, 'are those who keep their language efficient . . . keep it accurate, keep it clear.' [1]

Style can help your language become more efficient – i.e. achieve your target response.

Style for the ancient orators always had this practical purpose. 'Adornment of style', says Quintilian, 'contributes in no small degree to the success of a case.' [2]

Correctness is more than the avoidance of faults. Embellishment of style is something far more positive.

So what do we *mean* by style?

For the moment I shall use style in the sense of ornamental techniques which can be consciously employed by the presenter to help express his message.

These techniques must be appropriate – to the subject and to the presenter. Style in a courtroom must suit the advocate and more importantly suit the case. 'The advocate', says du Cann, 'does not live by style alone. Facts are the bricks with which he builds and style at best the mortar to bind them together.' [3]

Style is personal. 'Style is the man himself'. (Georges-Louis de Buffon, *Discours sur le style*.) The ornamental techniques you choose are those you feel happiest with. Luckily your choice is wide.

Choose correctly, be consistent, and the style becomes *your* style. An inevitability. A necessary part of you. An idiosyncrasy.

It will not happen at once. You will make incorrect choices as you experiment. You will feel unhappy with some techniques. The process may seem artificial. Of course. It is – at first. As all first learning steps are artificial. We begin by imitating and then adapting. The supreme test is fit. Does it fit us – and our purpose? But the more you practise the more it becomes part of you. Remember how long it took Mark Twain to prepare an impromptu speech.

Before we review the techniques, some words of warning. Technique must not get in the way of the message. It must assist it, if possible enhance it.

Avoid an image too grand for your subject. It will make *you* appear grandiose, or pompous or pretentious.

Avoid an image which leads you and your audience down a side road unless you know the way back. Avoid culs-de-sac.

Avoid a dead metaphor. Don't confuse familiarity with a 'shock of recognition'. The shock brings you up short. You recognize the connection. The recognition brings the nod. Familiarity brings the nodding off.

Keep the listener *busy*.

Avoid jargon. If your audience doesn't understand it you have generated language noise. If it's understood but seen to be élitist you have generated *psychological* noise.

Avoid over-rich words. They may contain 'unnecessary calories'.

Words are not fixed like numerals. Two always equals two. Written words contain ambiguities: spoken words even more. You must ensure that the secondary meaning is not conveyed, or that if it is, it has has no adverse effect upon the primary meaning.

A word has a **denotation** (i.e. the dictionary definition) and at least one **connotation** (i.e. an associated meaning connected with usage). The denotation is a statement. The connotation is more of a suggestion.

Even the most 'prosaic' text uses words with connotations. When you indulge in 'stylistic' speech the opportunities for ambiguity increase. Indeed that is one of its attractions.

Ambiguity is not all bad. A connotation may actually reinforce the denotation. A secondary and relevant meaning can enhance *your* argument. Provided you know that it's there. Provided *you* are in control.

Avoid uncertainty. Put statements in positive form. Check all your qualifiers. Are they necessary?

Use present, past and future tenses. Avoid conditional (would, could, should, may, might) unless you are absolutely certain you want to appear uncertain.

Be positive. Use the concrete rather than the abstract. Images are concrete.

Techniques

Warning. Do not use too many. Do not overdose. The first technique is particularly addictive:

Repetition

This aids the listener and aids the speaker. (It can be memorized.) It should be accompanied by a suitable gesture, e.g. a pointed finger or a fist hitting an open hand. Do not over-use.

'I have a dream.' (Martin Luther King)

Less obvious repetition can be very effective. A word or phrase is used early in the speech, repeated subsequently at decreasing intervals and used in the conclusion.

Variation

This is repetition using different words or phrases or examples. An accumulation of statements essentially conveying the same thing. Don't pretend anything else! Use it to reinforce rather than develop your argument.

Variation can be achieved by substituting one related *word* for another ('the bottle' for 'drink'); and using a part for the whole or the whole for a part ('shop floor' for 'factory', 'army' for 'soldiers').

Inversion

Reverse the normal sentence structure.

John F. Kennedy, 'Inaugural Address' (1961):

'Ask not what your country can do for you. Ask what you can do for your country.' (An overt form.)

Inversion is very effective at the end of repetition.

'We need to assemble our material. We need to organize our argument. We need to write like a talker. But above all – think like a listener. That's what we need to do.'

Sequence

Another aid to the presenter and listener. If possible announce it. The listener pricks up his ears, picks up his pen. 'There are three reasons.' 'What will happen in each of the next three months?'

Climax

The Romans refer to this as *gradatio* – reminding us to proceed gradually from one statement to another until the climax is achieved. There must be *at least* three stages. Repetition of a key word or phrase can help the sense of climax but it may be seen as a simple rabble-rousing technique. Remember that the secret of sentence structure is drama. Climaxes should abound in your script – not all of them major, of course.

Anticlimax

Very occasionally you can afford deliberate bathos, i.e. the build-up ends with a let-down, an incongruous finale. The audience has to know you meant it.

Irony

The trouble with irony is that the audience is unlikely to know you meant it. Avoid it till you reach the supreme champion stage.

Antithesis

On the one hand . . . on the other.

The complete body of the presentation may be one antithesis (e.g. pro and con) or a succession of antitheses.

Parallelism

Parallelism is similar to antithesis. The purpose, however, is to create not opposition but similarity. The similarity indeed may occur not in the thought but in the syntactical structure of the sentence.

Ellipsis

Remove words.

'Thank you' is an example of ellipsis. 'I thank you' sounds formal and unnecessary. Removing a verb may give more force. 'On to Berlin!', 'To err is human, to forgive divine.' We have already noted the increase in pace achieved by removing conjunctions.

Apostrophe

Here the presenter turns away from the audience and addresses someone else. The third party could be famous or dead or both; a character in fiction; or a specific member of the audience.

Understatement

Not stating too much because you know the audience will provide what is missing. All jokes (as we saw in Chapter 4) are understatement. The listener fills in.

Question

Questions invite participation. They prove that the presenter is aware of an audience. A question, as we have seen, can provide structural shape to a presentation. 'My Lords', said Edmund Burke in his indictment of Warren Hastings, 'what is it that we want here, a great act of national justice? Do we want a cause my Lords? . . . Do you want a criminal, my Lords? . . . My Lords, is it a prosecutor you want? [*note the use of inversion*] . . . Do we want a tribunal?'

These are *rhetorical* questions. The presenter is not expecting a spoken answer. The orator may hope for vocal support but *not* a conversation. Nevertheless he must be prepared for an articulate response. A heckler maybe or a raised hand.

The presenter may use a question to deal with an objection. He may play two roles. He can ask the question as an objector and answer it as himself. Or ask the question as himself and assume the voice of a 'supporter' answering it.

A question, a series of questions, can act as a useful signpost during the presentation. ('Where does that lead us?', followed perhaps by a glimpse of the answer.)

Cutting

Nothing improves style as much as cutting. Orwell's rule is 'If it is possible to cut a word out, always cut it out.'[4]

You can cut down as well as out by using short rather than long words.

Eliminate meaningless phrases (as a matter of fact, it seems to me, if you like, I feel it incumbent, I should add, at this juncture, etc.).

And remember Dr Johnson's advice (Boswell's *Life of Johnson*, 1773):

Read over your composition, and wherever you meet with a paragraph which you think is particularly fine, strike it out.

There is one caveat. Do *not* cut helpful redundancy. If the repetition enables the listener to keep on track, think twice before removing it.

Cut, in the same way you think, as a *listener*.

16 Noise

Language is a *code*. Remember that and you remember the listener.

Your script will be the victim of noise during presentation: your own delivery (voice and mannerisms); the attitude and behaviour of the audience; the incidental distractions (to eye and ear) in the room itself, in your dress, etc. We deal with these in **PIA**. Here we try to help you ensure that you *don't bring noise in with you*. In the script.

One of the best descriptions of noise occurs in a book on nonverbal communication. J. Lyons writes 'all utterances will contain a certain amount of information which, though signalled by the speaker, has not been "put there" by exercise of choice'.[1]

In other words you (the presenter) are responsible – though *not* intentionally. The question is – will you realize it before it happens, when it happens, after it happens or not at all?

Accidents, they say, don't happen by themselves. There are always contributory causes (plural). One of these causes is the listener himself.

We all practise selective perception. We see things we expect to see. We hear things we want to hear. Our background, upbringing and interests affect our interpretation. It is difficult to avoid such misconceptions. The listener has not switched off: he is participating. He is *constructively* misunderstanding. As Graves and Hodge put it, 'imaginative readers rewrite books to suit their own tastes'.[2] Listeners do the same with presentations.

The speaker provides the words. The listener provides the meaning. (In a sense of course that happens all the time. What we try to ensure is that the listener's meaning and the presenter's are identical, *shared*.)

In this chapter we review some of the chief causes of noise. Some we have met before. Some we shall meet again in **PIA**. The noise we guard against here is code (or language) noise. However, there are a few examples of psychological noise. See if you can spot them.

Circumlocution

Sentences, even whole paragraphs, go round the point without reaching it. By the time they do the listener may be hearing a different point altogether. Indeed, the presenter who speaks without a script may easily ad-lib his way into a new point.

Overlong sentences

Length by itself is not necessarily a bar to understanding. But a very long sentence must be well structured. The links must be visible.

Keep the subject, verb and object close together.

Avoid the suspended sentence in which qualifying phrases interpose between the subject and the verb or the verb and the object.

Avoid lists which put a strain on the listener's memory. 'Hand-held vacuum cleaners, spectral control photometric lenses, and advanced cushioning systems for sports shoes were direct spin-offs from the Apollo space programme.' Instead put the first subject next to the predicate and then introduce the second and third subjects. 'Hand-held vacuum cleaners were a direct spin-off from the Apollo space programme. So were . . .' etc.

Long words

Not all long words are difficult. Not all difficult words are long.

But always look for the shorter word. It acts as a discipline.

I remember at school being besotted with 'manifestly erroneous'. That was 'quite wrong' in morning dress.

Foreign words

A foreign word is fine – provided there is no exact English equivalent and the audience knows the word.

I know of no exact English equivalent for '*sympathique*'. But does the audience know it? What do I do? I use it – and try to give an approximation (without talking down).

'*O tempora, o morons!*'

Similarly if there is a choice between two English words try to use the Anglo-Saxon rather than the Norman. Start not commence. Climb not ascend. Send not transmit. As a rule Anglo-Saxon words are tougher and shorter.

Use English rather than foreign phrases.

Unconnected modifier

The modifier, you may gather, is not a popular fellow. He is better absent. When he does turn up he seems to attach himself to the wrong word.

'I usually go and see my mother on Sundays.'

Now *I* may know what I mean by that but how do I know that you do? Am I communicating that my usual routine on Sundays is to go and see my mother? Or that my usual day for seeing my mother is Sunday?

The way to make the meaning clear is to use different words – and avoid the modifier.

'Three Sundays out of four I go and see my mother.'
'Sunday is the day I go and see my mother.'

Words which sound the same

Conscious puns can enliven your speech. Apt puns can help put across major points. Unconscious puns can spoil a speech. A laugh in the wrong place unsettles the presenter and can affect other listeners who may not have seen a second meaning.

Not all second meanings are funny. In a way this is a pity since then there is no feedback to the presenter that something has gone wrong.

Words may both sound the same and be spelt the same. So even an accompanying visual may not help.

Unfortunate association

Eric is the best person to spot these.

Two thoughts come together and produce a bizarre picture.

Brown shot over the bar. The final whistle followed.

A BBC announcer referred to an incident at Heathrow concerning suspected illegal immigrants being returned against their will to Sri Lanka.

A dozen of the Tamils stripped and the captain refused to take off.

Brown shot over the bar.
The final whistle followed.

Malapropisms

It is easy to use the wrong word. In preparing a chapter I wrote 'punctuality' for 'punctuation'. Not all malapropisms are funny – as with words with more than one meaning, more's the pity. A return of signal is a warning.

At a conference on environmental pollution a speaker referred to the gradual build-up of chemical waste in a lake as a 'bombshell'. I spent a little while working out what he meant. The news would be a bombshell when it, say, exploded? Or was it already known – i.e. a 'bombshell' to the company, to those in the know? Then I realised he meant a 'timebomb'.

That half-minute spent correcting his script lost my attention. Noise.

Mixed metaphors

If the use of one image can cause confusion, the use of two closely together can cause havoc.

A mixed metaphor is evidence of thoughtlessness. The speaker has used image words without visualising them, clichés whose original pictures have faded. Even the incongruity of the juxtaposition may escape him:

The trouble is when I hung up my boots I threw the baby out with the bathwater.

If you employ what the *Reader's Digest* calls picturesque speech you need to see what pictures you are drawing in the mind of your listener.

Re-read your text for picture content. You will soon detect mixed metaphors by the bizarre illustrations.

A colleague once advised a meeting against too much self-promotion with these words.

'The trouble about blowing your own horn is that it can backfire.'

On BBC Radio 4 a correspondent reporting on the Syrian intervention in Beirut said 'The Syrians will be leaning over backwards to build bridges.'

Another radio interviewee said 'They are sitting on a powder keg. It could blow up in their face.'

Now – *they* know what they mean and you (as listener) know what they mean. So you could say communication has taken place. However, whilst you are contemplating the incongruous picture, you are paying no attention to what follows. Code noise has compromised simultaneous comprehension.

Imagery should illuminate – not eliminate – meaning.

Run-on sentences

Two thoughts, each perfectly sensible, collide. A connection is made between the two thoughts which is not intended.

Sentences can be classified (see p. 80) as expressing:

existence
co-existence
sequence
causation
resemblance

The presenter must take care that he has not accidentally reclassified his sentences. For example, in the following sentence *sequence* has become *causation:*

He turned on the radiator and fried some bacon.

In the following, *co-existence* has become *existence:*

Lecturer to hecklers: 'As soon as I stand up some fool begins to talk.'

Noise, then, is often the result of textual accidents. The presenter's familiarity with his subject acts as a barrier. He may write 'debtor nation' and be totally oblivious to the confusion registered in his audience. And remember patio door, the Irish singer?

Noise is a distraction. Moreoever, it reverberates. There are afterwaves. The listener may be waiting for new verbal accidents rather than attending to the subject. Stylistic mannerisms (e.g. the repetition of a phrase such as 'if you like', 'by the same token', 'so to speak'; or words which add nothing, such as 'personally', 'actually' or 'basically') can usurp the listener's attention. As can irrelevant asides, illogical connections or obscure references.

Alas, errors are too often not recognized until the performance. If the chair opposite is vacant and you can't find a critical friend to practise on, then tape your speech and play it back a day or two later without referring to the written text.

You may hear it anew. The innocent ear, listening like a listener.

17 Text into Script

We move now from **putting it together** to **putting it across**. In your hands is a text. In a week or so you will be standing up before an audience. In your hands will be a *script* or maybe key notes on a card.

From now on we are concerned not with what you want to say but how you should say it. The text has been structured with the listener in mind. The arguments have been ordered in the best way to combat the evanescence of time. Nevertheless the pages of type look daunting, remarkably like the manuscript of a book.

Your role is not to stand and read but *stand and deliver*.

A text inhibits delivery. A script aids it.

Do not confuse them. The written text is the prepared speech. It may be issued later as a reminder of what was said. It may even be printed. But it is *not* the script.

The script is for your eyes alone – and maybe for the event's producer and the projectionist if you are using visual aids. The script is a means to an end, not an end in itself. Its life is the duration of your presentation. It is a prop, a prompt, a friend in need. It will finish up annotated, coloured, underlined, highlighted – anything but tidy.

Make a duplicate copy of the text and file it for later reference. If possible have a new version of the text typed with double spacing between the lines. Check your paragraphs. If you feel you could make two paragraphs where one stood before, do so. If you can use a larger type-size so much the better.

And allow a wide margin on the left hand side. You will, inevitably, need it for additions, alterations and, above all, for indications of visual and audio aids.

What you are preparing is a working tool.

Now re-read the presentation. Aloud. As you intend to deliver it. Time your delivery.

It will almost certainly be over length. It will almost certainly be improved by cutting. The question is what do you cut?

That will be determined by the *point* of your presentation. Re-read it with the point in mind and a coloured pen in your hand. Put a dot against each paragraph which you feel contributes to the point you are making. Be honest.

John May, in his book *How to Make Effective Business Presentations – and Win!*,[1] suggests you mark every paragraph with one of three letters –E, N, D. That is E for Essential. N for Necessary. D for Desirable. The last category of paragraph is the first to go. He recommends using this technique on the platform itself. It may well be necessary. The preceding speaker may have overrun. You may have taken too long in your off-the-cuff preliminaries. You may have a question. So it is useful to mark potential deletions on your final script.

Nevertheless, you should try to ensure that the script represents the essential speech in as near perfect form as possible and to the correct length. It is better to delete superfluous material before you reach the podium – and to mark a number of items which could in an emergency also be sacrificed.

The rule is:
If in doubt – out.
It is also better to underrun than overrun.

You know as a listener that audiences can't take in too much. Quintilian advised 'not saying less but not saying more than is necessary'.[2] The traditional comedian's advice is worth remembering: always leave them wanting more. 'True eloquence', said La Rochefoucauld, 'consists of saying all that is necessary, and nothing more.'

Timing, of course, will be affected by visual aids. But not always in the same way. Key words screened simultaneously will aid the audience's assimilation of the message and therefore not add to the time taken, indeed may speed up the process. But an illustration of an individual point (e.g. a town plan) will demand more time for the audience to absorb the image and read some text.

Be very careful with timing. In my experience very few presenters arrive at a rehearsal knowing exactly how long their presentations will actually last. The major stumbling block is the visual aid. What they have timed inevitably is the spoken text alone.

There are various rules of thumb. 'A hundred words a minute if using visual aids' is one. The best rule of thumb, though, is *your own*. In other words rehearse, time yourself, check it with the actual performance. Repeat the process. Get more experience. Then eventually standardize on the format of script presentation you are happiest with. It may take a few years.

My own rule of thumb is two minutes a page. But I am not suggesting for a moment that that applies to anyone else.

You'll have gathered that this chapter is all about time. A script is essentially a text taken through time. The organization of the pages – the markings etc. – are simply means by which the speaker can deliver what he has to say so as keep the listener in step every second of the way from beginning to end.

A text is a journey through space at the reader's pace.
A script is a journey through time at the presenter's pace.

Look at Figures 1–3 below. Note that the text – what you write (Figure 1)

Figure 1   The text

```
Identity is, in our particular use of the term, the way we
present ourselves.  Corporate identity, therefore, is the way
the company presents itself.  There are strict guidelines.
These have been laid down by management in a corporate
design manual.

Corporate identity is a planned assembly of visual cues by
which the audience can recognize the company and
discriminate one company from another, and which may be used
to represent or symbolize the company.

So what is corporate image?  The dictionary defines image as
'a mental picture that someone, or people in general,
have of a person, company, organization etc'.  Corporate
image has been defined as 'the net result of the interaction
of all experience, beliefs, feelings, knowledge
and impressions that people have about a company'.
```

Figure 2   The script

<table>
<tr><td>Slide
IDENTITY</td><td>Identity is (in our particular use of the term) the way we present ourselves.</td></tr>
<tr><td>Slide
CORPORATE IDENTITY</td><td>Corporate identity, therefore ... is the way the company presents itself.

There are strict guidelines. These have been laid down by management in ...</td></tr>
<tr><td>Slide
CORPORATE DESIGN MANUAL</td><td>... a corporate design manual.

(pause)</td></tr>
<tr><td>Slide
AS TEXT</td><td>Corporate identity is a planned assembly of visual cues by which the audience can recognize the company and discriminate one company from another, and which may be used to represent or symbolize the company.</td></tr>
<tr><td>Slide
BLANK</td><td>So - what is corporate image?

The dictionary defines image as ...</td></tr>
<tr><td>Slide
AS TEXT</td><td>... 'a mental picture that someone, or people in general, have of a person, company, organization, etc'.</td></tr>
<tr><td>Slide
AS TEXT</td><td>Corporate image has been defined as 'the net result of the interaction of all experience, beliefs, feelings, knowledge and impressions that people have about a company'.</td></tr>
</table>

---

has been altered to make it the script (Figure 2), and then marked with cues (Figure 3). You will almost certainly find the text easier to read. That is as it should be – because a text is meant for a reader. The script, on the other hand, is meant for the speaker for whom those hieroglyphics have a special

Figure 3   The script marked with cues

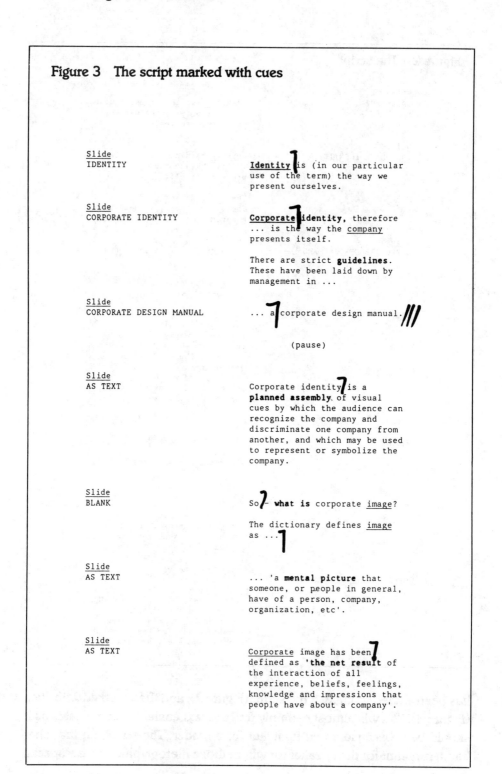

Slide
IDENTITY

Identity is (in our particular
use of the term) the way we
present ourselves.

Slide
CORPORATE IDENTITY

Corporate identity, therefore
... is the way the company
presents itself.

There are strict **guidelines**.
These have been laid down by
management in ...

Slide
CORPORATE DESIGN MANUAL

... a corporate design manual.

(pause)

Slide
AS TEXT

Corporate identity is a
planned assembly of visual
cues by which the audience can
recognize the company and
discriminate one company from
another, and which may be used
to represent or symbolize the
company.

Slide
BLANK

So - **what is** corporate image?

The dictionary defines image
as ...

Slide
AS TEXT

... 'a **mental picture** that
someone, or people in general,
have of a person, company,
organization, etc'.

Slide
AS TEXT

Corporate image has been
defined as '**the net result** of
the interaction of all
experience, beliefs, feelings,
knowledge and impressions that
people have about a company'.

significance. Those hieroglyphics will make it easier for the listener.

The more experienced you become in writing – to be heard – the less troubled you will be by departing from the accepted rules of punctuation. However, it may be necessary initially to alter the pattern of the text in order to aid delivery and therefore memory. (As you get more experienced you will automatically punctuate for delivery.)

Punctuation is crucial in a script. That may seem paradoxical since the listener can't see commas and colons and full stops. But what is punctuation after all? A collection of pauses, the graphic equivalent of drawing breath.

In **PIT** we saw how a long literary sentence is made colloquial by being broken down into a series of short sentences. However, if all sentences in a speech are short the effect becomes boring, even soporific. The speaker must vary the length – but without sacrificing meaning. He must therefore make sure that the connections between the parts of a longish sentence are clear and that the relationships are explicit.

Standard punctuation marks may not be sufficient for this task – particularly for the novice. The conventional use of these marks does not have the variety to accommodate the needs of the speaker.

For example, a comma may be used after each word on a list.

There are four aspects I wish to deal with: industry, economy, urban renewal and social welfare.

It may also denote a qualifying phrase.

The next topic I wish to discuss, and here I really need your participation, is the . . .

If you really know your script – and are an experienced speaker – you may be able to deliver both the above lines exactly as printed. However, to ensure that the listener really understands, you could mark the first piece in this way:

There are four aspects I wish to deal with//industry/economy/urban renewal/and social welfare.

The experienced speech writer will probably have written it thus:

There are four aspects I wish to deal with. Industry. Economy. Urban renewal. And social welfare.

The commas in the second piece should be indicated by brackets – to relate the qualifying phrase to the rest of the sentence.

The next topic I wish to discuss (and here I really need your participation) is the . . .

And the experienced script writer would of course already have included brackets rather than commas in his text.

Do not hesitate to mutilate your script with markings. Simple lines, brackets, underlining, circles will bring it to life, make the structure of the argument visible to enable you the better to communicate it.

The script makes the shape audible!

The script makes the
shape audible!

You may wish to invent your own marking. But you need to be consistent. Do not use one sign to represent two instructions. Similarly your colour coding must be consistent. The following are my own hieroglyphics.

1   /   Short pause.
   //   One-second pause.
            Longer pause. Unspoken emphasis. The listener is invited
   ///   to think about what you've just said.

2 **( )**   Brackets. For asides, qualifying phrases. Any slight departure from the main argument. A complete paragraph may be bracketed.

3 —————   Underlining. Spoken emphasis.

4 ①②③ etc.   Sections of the presentation – e.g. if the presentation is divided into distinct parts and the audience is told so, then it is crucial that you know where you are at any one time. The number is inserted against the appropriate paragraph and at the top of each page.

5 ———— /   Cue sign. Indicates the word on which the visual aid is shown or audio aid is played. This should be colour coded (e.g. red, slide; green, sound tape; blue, overhead acetate).

6 Video   Highlighting. The highlight pen is a great help. It allows you to bring key words to your notice immediately. I use it in the margin to indicate the visual or audio aid. Colour coded of course.

The highlight pen is also useful in the body of the text. I use a 'neutral' colour (yellow or pink, i.e. different from the colour code) and highlight the key words – say six a page. This enables me to know where I am when I return to the page. (Remember a speaker does not read his script. He *refers* to it. It is crucial to address the audience more than the script.)

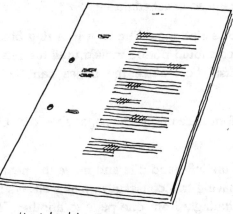

Highlight key words

Having key words highlighted means not only that you can reorientate yourself quickly when returning to the script (especially after an ad-lib or enforced absence) but that you can remind yourself of points that are coming up.

The script is your map of the course. You must at all times *know where you are*. If you compare the text with the script you will see that the former, because it is the same texture throughout, gives no indication of the shape of the speech, whereas the script is full of useful information and speaker-aids.

The spacing between lines in a presentation enables the speaker to distinguish one line from another. The increased spacing between paragraphs enables him to distinguish one paragraph from another. The further increased spacing between certain paragraphs (and maybe the numbering) enables him to identify new sections of the presentation.

The ample spacing between lines and in the margin – and at the top and bottom of the page – enables you to make notes on the day. The sudden late thought. A topical allusion. A comment provoked by something said by another speaker.

At the top of each page is an indication not only of the page you are on but of how many pages constitute the whole presentation – and therefore whereabouts in the performance you are.

You know how long the show should take. You can quickly estimate if you are on, behind or ahead of schedule.

If possible your script should be kept in a ring binder, or, failing that, stapled. The pages should not be moved until the final rehearsal. (A ring binder is obviously best since the pages can be returned after the rehearsal.)

During the performance proper the pages should be placed on the lectern in two piles.

You read from the left-hand pile and move the next page across when appropriate. By having two consecutive pages always in front of you you can move unhesitatingly from one page to another. Nothing irritates an audience more than the laborious turning of pages of the amateur speaker. Nevertheless, no matter how seamless your performance, you should try to avoid finishing a page in mid-sentence. Ideally each new page should begin with a new paragraph.

Don't worry if this means a lot of space at the bottom of the page. As I've said, the script is for your eyes only.

Form follows function. The script has no other purpose than to enable the speaker to deliver this presentation in as professional a way as possible. It has no afterlife. Paradoxically it succeeds best when it makes its own presence unnoticed. For the better it is constructed and marked the less the speaker has to look at it.

Well, you may say, if that's the case why have a script? Why not notes?

The more experienced speaker *will* rely on notes. He will of course incorporate the visual and audio aid indications and hieroglyphics. He will dispense with the aids to delivery since the speech will dispense with complete sentences. He may dispense as well with pages of A4, preferring to use cards (8 inches by 5: 203 mm by 127 mm). This way he may be able also to dispense with the lectern and hold the cards in his hand.

But, as we have noted, even the experienced speaker will have first *written the text.* That way he has first thought through and structured his argument and secondly structured his language.

And of course if he has done that then turning the written text into notes will be simplicity itself.

The beginner, however, is strongly advised to use a script.

But continued practice (indeed continual rehearsal with the one script) will enable the speaker to refer less and less to the written word. The well-marked script will enable him to deliver longer and longer sections of the argument without looking down: he will memorize the words or paraphrase them.

In effect the script, though complete, has *become notes*.

Many an accomplished presenter uses his script in this way. He has the total presentation there to refer to when necessary – and the highlighted, marked, coded shorthand version jumping out from the page. This enables him to speak spontaneously and maintain eye contact with the audience. He can more quickly establish rapport. He becomes more and more relaxed and can use the language appropriate to the occasion. The more he is in contact with the audience the more, obviously, it is in contact with him and the more it is made to feel that the presentation is uniquely relevant.

A script prepared in this manner – i.e. which can also be used as notes – will not come in between the transmitter and the receiver.

A text generates noise. A well-prepared script reduces noise.

18   Visual Aids – What For?

I hear I forget.
I see I remember.
I do I understand.

For the commercial presentation visual aids are the rule – not the exception. They help the listener become a viewer. And if they help him participate so much the better.

Note – they are aids for the *audience*. Not the speaker. Of course the words or images on the screen can also serve as a jolt to the presenter's memory. But their purpose is to assist the audience. The words on the slide must not serve as a text for the presenter to read from, nor should the audience be invited to read long passages. The screen should never become a wall newspaper.

Nor should it become the star performer. It may have its moments – but this is your show. The aids are means by which your argument is better understood by your audience. *You* are in charge.

The screen should never become a wall newspaper

And you must be in charge of your support material. This means ample rehearsal. But before that, of course, you must make the decision whether or not to use visual aids – and plan your presentation accordingly.

There *are* times when the visual aid is unnecessary: a short talk; an unsuitable occasion or location; a very small audience; an alternative means of reinforcing what you say is available (e.g. a printed handout), etc.

A small audience renders the visual aid unnecessary

These are exceptions.

Good visual aids will improve your presentation. They will improve your confidence. They will involve the audience. They will allow you to move more freely and (given a good sound system) walk away from the fixed podium.

Above all they allow you to treat the screen as a partner in your performance.

Clearly then, having decided to use visual aids, you must consider their use early in your preparation, i.e. once your argument has been structured and you begin writing the text. Indeed, if you leave a wide margin (or, as I do, write on the right-hand page only of an exercise book) you can drop in visual ideas as you proceed.

Because – and this role of visual aids is barely appreciated – the choice of an illustration helps you think through your argument. By summing up, say, a paragraph of text in one slide, you will focus your thoughts, maybe improve your use of language.

And if the visual can reduce confusion in your mind then it will certainly aid understanding in that of the audience.

Obviously a scientific or technical presentation is impossible without a mechanical drawing or statistical data. Explaining complex structural relationships is impossible without a chart of some sort. Try giving journey instructions without drawing a map (even with a finger in the air).

The most important use of visual aids therefore is as an *explanation*. The slide (or whatever) acts as **augmentation** of the presenter's text. Indeed the text is incomplete without it and its preparation has to be carefully devised. As has the delivery.

More usual are visual aids which act as **amplification**. These illustrate, reinforce, corroborate what the presenter is saying. A key word or sentence is projected. A difficult concept is made easier by simultaneously being heard and *seen*, or an abstract thought is made concrete. Or if two or three ideas are being discussed, or a list is mentioned, the visual aid can help keep the individual item in the audience's mind.

Another use of visuals is as **orientation**. You will recall the importance of signposts in the text. Similarly visual aids can act as markers. A presentation in four parts, for example, might list all four at the outset and each one at the appropriate part of the speech. Better still all four could be shown each time with the appropriate heading in a different colour.

'Mapping the course' is a good help to both presenter and audience. A preliminary handout with the section headings could perform this function. So could a permanent chart (e.g. on a blackboard or flipchart or even a

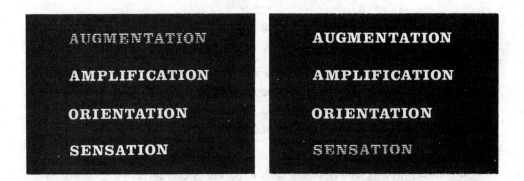

second screen). Much depends of course on the nature of the presentation. Should you wish to surprise the audience then such formality clearly would not be appropriate.

Surprise brings us to the fourth and final category of visual aid use, **sensation**. The visual is used for dramatic effect. The relevance of the subject may not be immediately apparent. The screen may be having an argument with the presenter, correcting him, muttering an aside to the audience. One presenter I saw in the US began his speech by saying he had been told to bring slides and then showed the 'only slides I have'. They were pictures of the kids on holiday. Sensation visuals need careful handling. They must not be over-used. But for involving the audience – waking them up in mid-presentation – they are most effective.

To sum up so far: visual aids are the rule rather than the exception. Their prime role is to help the audience during the performance. They help the presenter incidentally in performance – but primarily in preparing the presentation. They must be considered at the moment the presentation proper is structured. They serve four main functions:

> **augmentation:** part of the text
> **amplification:** reinforcement of the text
> **orientation:** text headings
> **sensation:** dramatic impact

19   Visual Aids – The Slide

There are various kinds of visual aid:

35 mm slide
overhead transparency
black- (or white –) board
flipchart
magnetic (or flannel) board
film
videotape
model

Slides are the most common and most practical. What follows applies directly to slides but has relevance for all visual aids. (We'll examine the overhead projector and other forms in the next chapter.)

Of course it is important to know as much about the room as possible prior to preparing your visual aids (see Chapter 22).

For example, if there is a large square screen you can then use both portrait and landscape (vertical and horizontal) images.

However, without it, you would be well advised to make all your slides landscape. Most screens *are* horizontal. Your slides will then hit the entire screen, whereas a portrait slide could go off top and bottom. To accommodate this the lens or projector will need to be adjusted. The result is that the image of every landscape slide is considerably reduced.

There is a minor drawback to the landscape-only rule: the portrait subject (e.g. a full-page advertisement or A4 illustration) is reduced in size, and has to be shown with a margin left and right. But it is a small price to pay for security and consistency.

The most important slide is a blank

Always carry half a dozen spare blanks. This might sound like a counsel of despair. One of your slides may have broken or have a mistake or have

The most important slide is a BLANK

been made redundant by a previous speaker. So you need to withdraw it from your presentation. Rather than leave the previous slide on too long, or come too quickly upon the next, or switch off the projector or (horror) let the projector show white light, you will need to project a blank – i.e. show a dark screen.

Do not be afraid of a dark screen. The choice is not between all-slides and no-slides. The rule for visual aids is – if in doubt, out. (We've met that before.) Some presenters feel they have failed if the screen is blank. The star of the presentation is the presenter not the screen. The screen is your associate.

If possible start with a blank

In a conference your introduction may be accompanied by a title slide: your name and topic. In which case leave it up there when you start. If you're in charge – start with a blank.

Establish contact with the audience first. Let the audience know that you're in charge. You may want to ad-lib, say something in response to the introduction or a previous speaker. A blank gives you freedom.

It also tells the audience not to expect the screen to dominate throughout – and to expect a subsequent occasion or two when the screen will again be blank.

Finally, it provides a moment of drama when the first slide goes up. You can add to the drama by incorporating topical details into the slide – e.g. the date, the occasion, the name of the audience.

Don't use too many slides

Does the visual *aid* ? If not what's it doing up there?

If there is no need for a slide then use a blank. Otherwise a succession of unimportant, unhelpful visuals will reduce the relevance and impact of the important slides. Drama will be lost.

Do not feel you have to fill the screen. Nothing bores an audience more than a succession of word-filled slides. They might just as well be given the text.

Project the slide for the right amount of time

There used to be a shaving cream, Erasmic, which was advertised with the slogan: 'Not too much, not too little, just right'. Assessing what's just right in terms of a slide duration will come only by practice. However, use every opportunity as a spectator to notice how long a slide remains on screen *in relation to the presenter's text.*

You will generally find that the majority stay on too long. There are occasions when presenters refer to a complicated chart, set of figures or mechanical drawing for too little time.

Don't leave slides on too long

The presenter may be nervous or afraid of boring the audience. He may assume that the audience will be as familiar with the material as he is. Mostly, though, the inexperienced presenter leaves a slide on after it has made its point.

The audience, of course, will still be looking at it. Maybe reading the words whilst the presenter is speaking other words. Maybe worrying about the use of language – even making anagrams, or setting the text to music.

A slide projected too long – or too short – is *noise*.

Blanks eliminate noise.

One picture is worth a thousand words

And that's not always a good thing. In the right place, at the right time and for the right length of time, the right picture is invaluable.

However, some presenters leave a picture on too long in preference to a blank in the belief that unlike words, which may conflict with the spoken text, a picture will act as a neutral setting for the eye to rest on.

This is a fallacy. The longer a picture stays on the more the audience sees in it. Indeed they may believe you want them to look *into* the picture. After all you put it up there. (A cartoon, for example, should never be overexposed.)

One picture may be worth a thousand words – but nine hundred of these may be entirely irrelevant.

You and the screen – a double act

The visual aid is an associate. It frees you up. Don't let it freeze you.

You must remain in charge. You must be seen to be in charge.

Occasional reference to the screen is natural and necessary. Every so often you need to know that the right image is being projected. But constant reference loses contact with the audience. It's also rude. It tells the audience that you're nervous. Particularly (and I've seen this many times) when the presenter actually looks at a blank screen!

On the other hand, when you are in command of your material then the occasion when you *do* refer to the screen – maybe walk up to it – can be very effective. For example, when there are charts or diagrams which you need to take the audience through. You need to establish a triangle: you, the screen and the audience.

Explain the chart. Tell the audience, for example, what the horizontal and vertical axes represent. Tell them the figures to notice in particular. If possible use a laser pointer.

When you achieve mastery of the medium you can then risk leaving the other two parts of the triangle alone together. Pause. Let the audience study the screen for a few seconds.

But use that time. Drink some water. Watch the audience. Suck up feedback. Don't turn your back. Remain in charge.

Make the slides coherent

By 'coherent' is meant not simply understandable (that goes without saying – though not all visual aids are) but consistent. The presentation must be single-minded not only in message but in style. Each slide must look part of the one presentation.

If at all possible do not use slides from previous presentations.

The choice of lettering and illustration must be relevant to the subject, the occasion, the audience.

Make the slides visible

True story: at a conference a few years ago a presenter was listing the key criteria for a public relations programme. He chose to display red lettering against a red background. He paused at one slide and apologized for the poor illumination. The key word we had difficulty in seeing was the word . . . 'visibility'.

There is no golden rule for the colour of type or lettering. But there is a yellow rule. **Yellow out of black**. The contrast is excellent. Black out of yellow is not quite as good.

I prefer to use reversed-out type (i.e. a black background) as opposed to a dark type on a white or pale background, since the pale background shows the dirt. Slides attract a lot of static.

Avoid pastel colours. Avoid too many colours. Make sure that the colours are consistent.

Coding is important – not only for colours but also typeface and type-size. When planning your word slides make sure that they relate exactly to your text. For example, should you decide simply to show some dozen key words or phrases, each of which is equally important, then adopt the same typeface, type-size and colour. Upper and lower case is preferable.

Should you wish to use more visual aids, e.g. to illustrate your section headings and certain phrases from the text, then make sure the audience recognizes your code. The headings in capitals, say, and the phrases in upper and lower. The typeface should be constant. The headings should be in large size or a different colour. There is considerable choice. But once chosen, the code must not change. You establish the conventions. If you keep to them you help the audience. If you don't you create noise.

Make the layout work

If you remember the audience, you can't go wrong.

The layout should be balanced but not always so symmetrical or identical that the change of slide may go unnoticed!

Align the text from the left-hand side. Also remember that the top of the screen is more likely to be viewed by everyone in the audience than the bottom.

Make the words and pictures as large as you can.

If you want to show a lengthy piece of text (over thirty words), then use two consecutive slides with a larger type-size rather than one with a smaller.

Images should wherever possible and appropriate occupy the entire projection area.

Do not try to put too many thoughts or images on to one slide.

Ideally put one idea across per slide. If you must put across two or more ideas make certain the dividing line is clear – and understood. (This may need a little rehearsal. Whereas presenters often practise their words on a colleague, they rarely practise their slides.)

If you use large type and small type on the same slide, then the reason for the difference must be obvious – to you as well as to the audience. Presumably the larger type means the more important point.

Type height should never be less than one eighth the height of the total slide. This is not to suggest that you should aim for eight lines a slide. More than six and you're in trouble. Always use line spacing.

The typeface should be simple, clean and easy to read from the back of the hall.

Again the choice is amazing. But don't be carried away. Your guide should be the public signs you see on buildings and highways – and especially on motorways. Clear sansserif faces with few fripperies and no change in thickness. Don't be seduced by a type book – indulging yourself like a small child given the freedom of a sweetshop. Just stick to simple faces and then, when you wish to create a sensation, introduce a statement in Gothic or Cheltenham Bold.

Cheltenham Bold
Serifs

GOTHIC
Sans serif

A pictorial slide must contain one dominant item. It is more likely to make an impact on the audience if it is centrally placed or near the classical golden mean.

Two or three items can of course be shown but the composition must be carefully arranged. The dominant item can overlap a subsidiary item.

Make your visuals colourful but not garish. And don't introduce too many colours, either on a single slide or in the total presentation.

And finally, make sure that the slide is *dynamic*.

Some presenters avoid word slides altogether. I'm not such a purist. Though I would agree that too many presenters use too many, some use nothing but, and some put virtually everything worth saying on slides. The only excuse for the last is an audience whose English is at best a second language.

Key words, headings, essential phrases, difficult ideas, difficult words . . . these are helped by verbal slides.

Abstract words are not. Abstract words are helped by images.

John May makes a useful point:

Go for the greatest impact. Visuals become stronger as they move on from figures to graphs, to diagrams, to pictures, to objects, and to actions. If you want a visual to hit hard, take it along this path as far as the basic idea can be persuaded to go.[1]

20 Visual Aids – The Other Aids

The omnipresent slide projector often blinds us to the potential of the more ordinary forms of visual aid. Let's put the record straight.

Blackboard

The great advantage (shared by the whiteboard) is spontaneity. It requires little preparation. A diagram can be created piecemeal. You can take the audience along with you. The key headings (map of the course) can be shown throughout the presentation.

The disadvantage, of course, is that you must turn your back on the audience as you write or draw. You then have to decide if you talk as you chalk. A blackboard cannot be used in a room bigger than a classroom.

But it's very simple – and has stood the test of generations.

Flipcharts

Do not use a flipchart simply as a blackboard. If you do then all the above disadvantages apply – and on a small surface area. Flipcharts can be used for spontaneous image and message graphics and simultaneous presentation but are best used when properly prepared. Some charts can be complete. Others can be pencilled in for the presenter to thicken or crayon at the time.

Sheets can be thrown over the back of the easel, still attached, or torn off and thrown on the floor. Though very dramatic the first couple of times, the gesture palls and the effect is messy. Far better to tear out the important charts and pin or Blu-tack them around the walls.

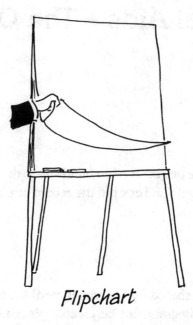

Flipchart

One trick for the presenter who does not want to tear out the charts is to present in the reverse order – i.e. count the number of charts you need (lettering or pencilling where you will) and then toss them over the back of the board. When you start you simply *bring down* the first chart and so on.

But the flipchart is not to be recommended for a large gathering or long presentation.

Magnetic (or flannel) boards

Again this is for the small room and the informal presentation.

Its magic ingredient is its ability to hold individual sections of a visual and allow the presenter to build up a total picture piece by piece.

It is easy to use. And easy to misuse.

It demands far greater preparation and rehearsal than the previous aids in this chapter.

The presenter must begin at the end – since the point of his presentation is the ultimate visual. With this in mind he must then work out exactly how each component is pieced together – and when.

If it is important to know you have slides before writing your speech it is *crucial* to know that your aid is a magnetic or flannel board. The board determines the final structure of your presentation.

Obviously such a board demands that the material is prepared well in advance. Its *raison d'être* is the build-up. Merely putting up and taking down isolated words or simple sections is a misuse of the technology.

The board is limited in use and allows little if any spontaneity. But visual commentary – within its limits – can be quite effective, especially if the finished image needs to remain in view for some time.

Film and Videotape

Videotape has largely supplanted film. However, film has greater clarity and can exploit a bigger screen than videotape.

The drawback is the dominance of the projector and literal noise. Also the room has to be darkened.

Video today is a more usual experience for the audience. The size of the screen depends of course on the size of the room. A classroom can be served by two or three monitors (i.e. domestic receivers). Anything bigger demands a special projection device (such as Barco 3) and/or a batch of monitors. Video, of course, does not need a darkened room.

Video projector

But both film and video suffer from one major disadvantage. The machinery takes over – less so in the case of video, since most presenters are accustomed to operating a home video recorder and can stop, pause or if necessary rewind.

Nevertheless the machinery does assume a very important, probably even a dominant, role. The presenter may lose contact with the audience. It is advisable to employ an operator.

Much will depend upon the scripting, the context in which the tape or film is shown. Do not say 'I thought you might like to see a few commercials', or 'As a change from my voice here's something a little more exciting.'

In other words do not abdicate.

Instead try to give the audience something to do while viewing. For example, 'Drama is about tension. Compare the lack of tension in the first clip with the heightened tension in the second. What contributes to the effect?'

Overhead projector

John May has called the OHP 'the presenter's friendliest visual aid'.[1]

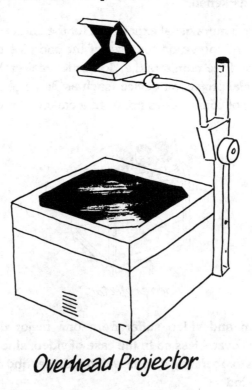

Overhead Projector

You write or draw on a light table in front of you and the words and pictures shine out on the screen behind and above you . . . You present in normal lighting, but work with a bright image. You don't have to turn your back (as with flipcharts or chalk board), and can easily maintain eye contact with your audience. You can switch on or off as you like.[2]

One great advantage of the OHP is also its main disadvantage – the size of the image. Any imperfection on the acetate is not only magnified on the screen but, since acetates are transparent, every speck of dust will make itself known.

Of course special acetates can be prepared in advance (as with slides – white out of black) but somehow I feel that loses the essential characteristic of the OHP, its spontaneous character. Whereas the slide is an associate, the OHP is an *extension* of the presenter. The situation May so feelingly describes is the heart of this system. The presenter is communicating via the acetate with his audience.

The visual is always 'in sync.'. It and the speech happen simultaneously. The presenter and subject are integrated. The presenter and audience proceed together.

However, the ease with which a professional presenter uses the OHP should not delude us into regarding the machine as simple to operate. It is simple if nothing is demanded of it short of an instant scribbling pad or a substitute slide show.

The OHP is far more than that. It allows the presenter to *build up* – far more simply and effectively than the magnetic or flannel board, for instance – and to *take away*.

Items can be hidden. Items can be revealed. Subtle effects can be achieved.

The presenter can combine elements. He can show a prepared visual and add to it, or alter it. He can point to something on it (never point to the screen itself) with a pointer or a pencil (never your finger) and if necessary leave the pointer in place.

He can switch off, put a new acetate in place, speak without using the OHP, then switch on again to reveal a new image at exactly the right moment.

He can even superimpose an image from an OHP on to that from a slide projector!

All this takes practice.

So does the creation of messages and images in front of the audience. All the rules for slides are appropriate here. They are harder to keep when performing live. The images must be simple, and tidy. The colours must be bold.

Acetates can be prepared in advance using a felt-pen or a typewriter. Special carbon-backed white paper can be used – resulting in reversed-out type. Or original art or typescript can be photocopied on to suitable acetates.

But prepared acetates should be *thoroughly* prepared, i.e. they should be fixed in cardboard frames. Manufacturers provide these – at some cost. They are easier to handle. Unframed acetates stick to each other. They are sold in covering film to prevent contact. But the film has to be removed prior to use. Doing that just before you project ensures less static on the acetate but takes up valuable time.

Some machines allow you to use a continuous roll of acetate film. This is cranked across the light table as you need it. The roller can go either way so you can reshow a recent image. However, it is best to proceed in one direction only – though two-way functioning allows you to prepare images in advance.

Physical objects

An actual *thing* may be more dramatic and meaningful to the audience than a slide showing it. If the object is small then a slide could be projected simultaneously for those in the back rows.

For example, you are speaking on the cost of oil. So much a barrel. 'What exactly is a barrel? This is . . .'

Large objects may pose problems in the bringing on and taking off. And they must never outstay their relevance.

Objects focus attention. So do working models and demonstrations.

*An actual thing to show
may be more dramatic
than a slide*

They also demand rehearsal and faith.

There is one speaker-aid which can inspire confidence in the presenter though it may reduce it in the audience – **autocue**. A narrow sheet of large-type text is projected on to either one clear glass screen in front of the lectern or two screens angled inwards from each side of the lectern at the presenter's eye level.

The presenter reads. The audience has an unobstructed view – indeed, may not even notice the screen(s) or realize that the presenter is reading.

This is virtually the same technique employed by television news readers. (In their case the text is projected on the camera lens.) The trick is to pretend you're not reading, to pause, move your head, and avoid the fixed stare.

It is crucial to rehearse. The text has to be transferred to the sheet and must be checked. The presenter must speak the text in full and work closely with the autocue operator – particularly regarding pauses, possible ad-libs, changes of pace, etc. Otherwise the speed of the presentation may be determined not by the speaker but by the operator!

Autocue is something of a paradox. It is used best by experienced speakers who probably don't need it. Inexperienced speakers, on the other hand, tend to rely on it totally and thus effect a wooden, transfixed delivery.

Only a professional can use autocue and still maintain contact with the audience.

Audio Aids

Occasionally sound can come to the aid of the presenter. A taped voice or piece of music is a dramatic change of texture provided, of course, it is clearly audible.

Be especially careful with speech. The audience will not have the benefit of the speaker's mouth movements or a visual context to guide it. Short bursts of vocal comment work best. Similarly, short snatches of music can point up an argument or serve to indicate a new stage of the presentation.

A sound effect could revive the audience.

Audio aids work best when short, telling and relevant. They work worst when the audience has to work hard at listening and when they take too long. The audience does not know where to look. So if the tape lasts fifteen seconds or over, project a slide to focus attention.

Quotations on slide can be accompanied by a taped voice as a change from that of the presenter.

But the most effective form of audio aid is performed by the audience itself. Singly or together. For example, in a presentation on communication they can be asked to read a caption from the slide (one which contains a mistake which most people don't notice – thus proving we see what we expect to see). Or a word is screened for which there is more than one accepted pronunciation (e.g. 'ambivalent') or which is pronounced differently in the north and south of the country (e.g. 'scone'). Or you give one volunteer a group of words to speak and ask the other to write on the OHP what he is saying.

Audience participation is the key to the use of any aid, aural or visual. The aid must be appropriate to the subject, the occasion, the audience, the location – and the presenter.

We now need to examine the relationship between visual aid and presenter more closely.

21 Visual Aids – Relationship with Presenter

If you think of the screen as a partner, albeit a junior one, you will not treat your visual aids as an afterthought.

If you decide to use visual aids then you must plan a double act from the beginning.

Imagine then how you would plan your show if you had co-opted a flesh and blood junior partner . . .

What would you do first? You would allocate roles. You might subsequently change or switch. But you would make sure that the audience understood, i.e. understood the convention you had adopted.

What relationship would you effect? There is a limited choice, though the room for manoeuvre is ample.

With two protagonists Presenter (P) and Screen (S) you have but four options:

(1) P alone
(2) S alone
(3) P supported by S
(4) S supported by P

Most presentations consist of (1) and (3).

Remember the slide should *show* rather than say. That's why it's called a *visual* aid. You are the talker. The aid is the demonstrator. It's important to establish that convention at the earliest opportunity. The audience must know that – and must also know that you are the senior partner.

Not only must you declare your relationship with the audience at the earliest moment, you must also make plain your and its relationship with the screen.

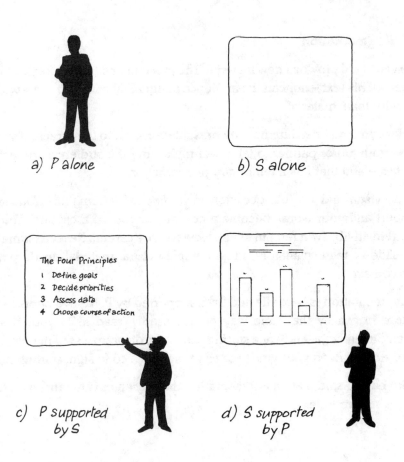

a) P alone

b) S alone

The Four Principles
1 Define goals
2 Decide priorities
3 Assess data
4 Choose course of action

c) P supported
   by S

d) S supported
   by P

The screen, the projector, the arrangement of the room . . . all are sending out signals, expectations. Satisfy them as quickly as possible. Don't have the audience waiting for visuals that aren't there. If you don't intend using visuals throughout your presentation then introduce a blank early on. Act fair. You can always surprise later. But unless you establish your conventions you have no norm against which to surprise.

As we saw in a previous chapter slides serve four functions:

(1)   **augmentation**
(2)   **amplification**
(3)   **orientation**
(4)   **sensation**

(1) Augmentation

The visual aid provides *new* material. The presenter cannot do justice to one aspect of his text – nor can the audience adequately comprehend – without the additional material.

Here you may risk handing the presentation over to the screen. If you do allow your junior partner to take over make sure the audience appreciates the fact – and that it is a temporary phenomenon.

The visual aid on this occasion is *additional information*. You are in support and your words become a commentary, even a caption. You can afford to ad-lib, even remain silent. However, be careful. Never assume that the slide is self-explanatory. Most complex visual material needs putting into context.

Augmentation is best effected by S supported by P. No two people see a picture in exactly the same way or necessarily 'read it' in your desired order. Similarly the audience staring at a chart, diagram, list of figures, road map, etc. will need your guidance as to meaning, code sign, starting point.

But having said that, in augmentation the presenter is in (and seen to be in) the support role.

(2) Amplification

This is the usual function of visual aids. The visual aid, without adding new information, provides *added meaning* to the material presented in the text. It does so by *reinforcing* the message – i.e. duplicating it, involving two senses (sight as well as sound); or *paraphrasing* the message (e.g. showing an alternative to the words expressed); or even *complementing* the message (i.e. extending its meaning by a new example).

An abstract word can be illustrated or a concept can be illuminated by an image.

The visual can explain a comment. It can focus. If the presenter speaks about a man in a boat and it matters whether it's an admiral in a destroyer or a North American Indian in a canoe then the slide will fix it for the audience. If it does not matter – or if the presenter can explain sufficiently in the text – then do *not* show a visual.

Do not show a visual aid for the sake of showing one.

The projection of identical text should, as I've suggested, be used sparingly, e.g. where there is something particularly important or difficult to be conveyed.

But should you speak what you show? At crucially important times, yes. But always leave enough time for the audience to read the slide for itself. Otherwise you will be thought patronizing.

A key word can be shown to make sure the audience focuses on the really important fact in the accompanying passage of text.

(3) Orientation

Here the visual aid tells the audience where they are – in the presentation, in the argument. The slide is simply a landmark. The presenter could leave it on the screen. If the presentation is in distinct sections a short pause, even a sound tape musical interlude of a few bars, can mark the presentation's progress.

But try to do more than call the sections Part 1, Part 2, etc. Provide titles which suggest the stage of the argument, illustrate development. Or, if the slide says 'Part One', then complement it in the commentary.

The fundamental virtue of a visual aid is that it helps the listener's *memory*. Unlike a reader he cannot go back and re-read. The slide can keep a cumulative score and direct the argument, consolidating what has been said.

(4) Sensation

Here the screen is used for impact. But the surprise is relevant.

It will have become obvious, I hope, that the relationship of presenter and visual is a complex one. Although the partners progress in step, they do not simply echo each other. First one takes the lead, then the other. First one takes the stage alone, then the other.

In the early days of TV advertising, agency creative people were taught that in commercials you should 'say what you show and show what you say'. This was of limited use. If you showed a bowl of soup and accompanied it with a voice-over saying 'this is a bowl of soup', then either the video or the audio was redundant. If you showed a bowl of soup and the announcer mentioned the variety and brand, then further relevant information was being transmitted. But if you showed the soup and a voice-over off screen said 'Is this home-made?' or 'What do you call this rubbish?', then a tension was created between the picture and sound and the viewer was involved. You had drama.

Similarly the slide can create a tension by 'commenting' on the text, even contradicting it.

Dramatic touches maintain audience interest.

The screen can perform unaided. Often a cartoon can say something more immediately and with greater impact than the presenter. It invites, even demands, the participation of the audience. The presenter intervenes at his peril.

But of course the presenter can also perform unaided. To repeat: don't assume because you have, say, a slide projector that you have to have images continually on the screen. You yourself are a visual aid – as we shall see when we discuss delivery.

The visual aid prevents the presenter from saying too much.

Conversely the presenter prevents the visual aid from showing too much.

The visual aid affects the pace of the presenter's delivery. You must allow time for the image to register. This means you may go more slowly during slides. This can be disconcerting for the audience if you then proceed rather quickly when there's no visual aid. On the other hand, to maintain a steady unchanging pace can be tedious. Avoid 'metronome' delivery.

Occasionally a visual aid should be used to bring you and the audience up short, cause you to pause. Maybe you should leave the lectern and look at it, point at a feature, read out some text. Every so often let three or four slides illustrate one point.

Use any device to introduce light and shade.

Remember finally – it's a double act. The presenter provides the context for the visual. The visual provides the context for the presenter.

22 The Room

Most presentations take place in the wrong rooms. The room may have been built for one purpose, is being used every day for a second and is now adapted for a third – your presentation.

Take this as a rule – you will not present in ideal conditions. At least this way you will be prepared (and should the conditions be perfect, pleasantly surprised) and you will make it your business to look the room over.

...as a rule, you will not present in ideal conditions

You have prepared your presentation. The text has been structured – and visual aids have been made to assist understanding. All that preparation is under threat from the noise created by the room itself. It is inconceivable for a presenter to present well cold, i.e. in a totally strange environment.

Ideally of course you should play at home, in your own purpose-built presentation room. This will eliminate 90 per cent of surprises.

But even playing away you may still be able to influence the organization of the room if you act soon enough.

You should enquire about the room as soon as you are invited to speak. If you are the only speaker then the organizers should respect your need to familiarize yourself with the location. If you are one of several, e.g. at a conference, then the organizers should be holding a preliminary getting-to-know meeting. Note that this is not a rehearsal, which will take place later – often too late for your purposes. If no such meeting is envisaged, ask to see the room, preferably in use. Watching other people perform will soon alert you to the potential advantages and disadvantages of the environment.

Just as you need to know whom you are talking to, so you need to know the conditions in which they will be attending. All this, ideally, before you prepare your presentation. Though it may seldom work out like this, you should always be ready to adjust your presentation to accommodate the accommodation.

For example, if you are the only speaker, and you wish to involve a smallish audience in a free-ranging discussion, then a formal seating plan will undermine your plans. Conversely, if your presentation veers towards showbiz then a random collection of tables and chairs will suit your intention less well than theatre-style seating.

Let us suppose for a moment you *could* have complete control of the room. What would you decree?

You can be seen by everyone.
You can see everyone.
You can be heard by everyone.
You can hear everyone.
Everyone – including you – should be in reasonable comfort.

(Not much to ask, you might think. Then think back to your experiences as a delegate.)

Assuming you know the approximate size of the audience, what size room should you go for? Antony Jay would opt for one slightly smaller than necessary rather than one distinctly too large. Empty spaces are depressing. He cites Winston Churchill who 'insisted that the rebuilt House of Commons should not have as many seats as there were MPs'.[1] A few people occasionally standing in the aisles would be a small price to pay.

Nevertheless, I would opt for a little extra room rather than risk too close a proximity between the speaker and audience and, especially, among

CONFERENCE ➡

Having overpriced it at £300 per head, we're undersubscribed with 20 seats per bottom

members of the audience, always provided the empty chairs can be stowed and the unoccupied section of the room can be closed off or given some alternative role (e.g. as a display area or for subsequent refreshments).

The key to size is *comfort*.
Discomfort equals noise.
And an uncomfortable audience lays the blame on the presenter.

Alas, presenters are often unaware of the conditions in which their talks are received. How rarely do speakers at a conference stay the whole day! And on the stage, behind the podium, amidst all the excitement of the show, a presenter could be forgiven for thinking the heat he feels is self-generated . . . or, conversely, that because he is warm there is no icy blast from the malfunctioning air conditioning.

The pattern greeting you may be the result of a previous meeting

The rule in **PIT** – think like the listener – applies equally in **PIA**.

If possible check the ventilation. But above all check the arrangement of the chairs.

Treat nothing as sacrosanct. The pattern greeting you may be the result of a previous meeting, or the usual means of arranging the room for maximum attendance. Enlist the help of the caretaker or producer.

A room a little too big does allow you flexibility to arrange the seating to suit your purpose and, given time, the opportunity to experiment with alternative patterns. As already suggested, the arrangement should be determined by the type of presentation you intend to give.

If informal and participative – a seminar for a dozen people – then theatre-style seating is clearly counterproductive. Indeed the whole thrust suggested by the arrangement of the room may blind you to its potential. Remove the chairs (if only in your mind) and consider alternative focal points.

Freedom to change the shape of the room can help you ensure that the doors are in the right place – i.e. not too near the presentation area and that latecomers arrive at the back of the room.

The small group could form a *circle* with the presenter as part. That is if *you* want to be part of the group. It is ideal for a participative session, for questions and answers, but less suitable for the projection of visual aids.

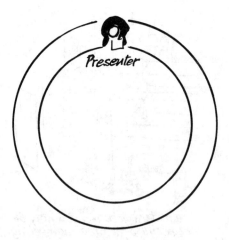

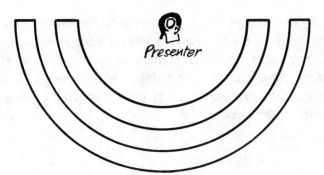

More suitable is a *horseshoe*. This puts the presenter in pole position but still encourages discussion. Twenty chairs can easily be accommodated in a single semicircle. So everyone is in the front row and in the show. With more people then use two rows, staggered either in a semicircle or a shallow double V.

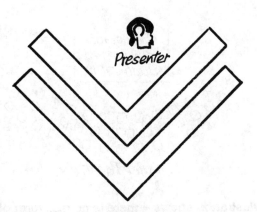

One of the advantages of non-theatre seating – circle, semicircle, horseshoe, shallow V – is that people feel less intimidated. They have room to stretch their legs. They can see others without feeling the others' eyes on the back of their necks. Similarly the presenter is able to communicate easily with all the delegates, even when sitting down.

Each of these informal plans allows each delegate to have a small writing surface in front of him. Ideally of course the decision should be the presenter's. Do you want the audience to write, to make notes? If so then make sure some small tables are provided. However, a table can act as a convenient repository for individual noise: a newspaper, office correspondence, the making of notes totally unrelated to the presentation.

Theatre-style seating plans are more suitable for formal presentation and particularly for show-biz. And are inevitable once the audience is larger than forty. They assist the presenter in the projection of visual aids. There is almost always a stage or at least a dais. Unfortunately it is seldom high enough for the back rows to see everything. Staggered seating is essential though not the entire answer.

But – as the illustration shows – there is no one form of theatre seating. Taking the National Theatre as our guide you can always adopt the Olivier as a change from the Lyttelton. The Olivier is more 'democratic'. The National audience may not exactly join in but entrances and exits are made from all parts of the theatre. Similarly if you arrange your seating wide and shallow you will encourage greater audience involvement.

Again, the choice is yours.

The purpose of this rapid tour of seating plans is to remind you first of your options and second of the need to consider the room at the earliest possible stage in preparing your presentation.

Communication is two-way. What do you want your audience to *do*?

Meanwhile how about the presenter? What sort of performance do you intend? It *is* a performance, remember. Although you will try to be yourself, the situation is artificial. It is not usual to project your voice, to speak to so many people at once or to speak for so long. Anything you can do to eliminate mistakes, to familiarize yourself with the surroundings, to make yourself at ease, will make sure that the 'you' who is presenting is recognizably that 'you' you would like it to be.

What relationship do you wish to effect with the individual in the audience? Pedagogue and pupil? Guru and disciple? Are you a coach, a *primus inter pares*, 'one of the boys'?

Clearly the same room format cannot be right for all of them.

What about the lectern? Do you need one? If you are giving a formal presentation and/or using visual aids which you operate yourself then probably you do. If your script is in the form of cards you may not. If you have a neck mike, or the acoustics don't require any sound amplification, then you can move freely and use the lectern merely as a base. (Too many presenters use it as a refuge!)

sanctuary!

The lectern is a speaker's aid. Too often it becomes a barrier (noise) between the presenter and the audience. It is the desk between the boss and employee, the teacher and the pupil. Is that what you want? Perhaps you could stand at an angle to the lectern? Or move away to operate the OHP?

But unless you know the conditions of the room, how can you begin to make these decisions?

You must acquaint yourself with the room before you speak. Even if it's only half an hour before. That will give you time enough to check the equipment (see Chapters 29 and 30 on rehearsal); the sight lines (when one speaker-aid such as a flipchart is actually interfering with another, such as the screen); the exits and entrances; the lectern (and angle it into the central stage so you don't have to turn your head to look at the screen); the seating arrangements (and with luck stagger the chairs); get the feel of the place by standing where you will be standing and by sitting where they will be sitting.

One final word about the room. What will it look like *finally*, i.e. when your presentation is over? For example, if there is a question and answer session for fifteen minutes what will the audience be looking at? A blank screen? A darkened stage? A mess of acetates? A flipchart which accurately sums up your message?

Will the room be part of the message?
Or will be it noise?
Context is a primary element of communication.
The room is your context.

You may be glad it's over, but don't leave the presentation area looking like this

23 Delivery

Rhetoric was defined by Quintilian as 'the science of speaking well'.[1] It comprised five parts: invention (of material), arrangement (of the divisions of the speech), expression (or style), memory and *delivery*.

> Language of but moderate quality, if recommended by forcible delivery, will produce a more powerful effect than the most excellent language, if deprived of that advantage.[2]

Your message, then, is affected by your delivery. **PIT** is affected by **PIA**. No matter how carefully you have structured your argument and your language for understanding, your delivery and the surroundings in which it takes place will modify your message. As Hawkes says 'Meaning . . . resides in the total act of communication.'[3]

That total act provides ample opportunity for noise. Though noise may have been eradicated in the script, an irritating mannerism by the speaker, a misreading of a gesture by or from the audience or a mishandling of the equipment will, in the words of the communications scientist, 'diminish the integrity of the signal' and totally undo the careful preparation.

This chapter and the following three on delivery, though inevitably overlapping in content, deal broadly with three main factors, three means of reducing noise: control of your audience; control of your material and equipment; and, to begin with, control of yourself.

You will be nervous.

That isn't at issue. The only question is *how* nervous? Don't be ashamed. Why shouldn't you be nervous? You're putting your reputation on the line every time you stand up and talk. You may have checked everything and the unexpected may happen. If you have something new to say then how can you know how it will be received? Start listing all the problems and you have every reason to be nervous.

Keep control of your audience

But most professional presenters (indeed most leading actors) remain nervous no matter how experienced. Nerves stimulate adrenaline. The professional will tell you that his bad performances coincided with lack of tension. He may actually worry because he is *not* nervous!

Now he may welcome nerves but he still has to control them and he must not let the audience know. And there is no reason why it should – as this chapter makes clear.

The first requirement for a novice speaker is to listen. Listen to other speakers and observe not only the speaker's delivery but the way the rest of the audience is reacting to the presentation. You will learn from every presentation, from the amateur as much as the professional. Gauge each speaker. Ask yourself what differentiates the good from the bad. The really proficient speaker is in control. He gives the impression that if his script or notes disintegrated, if the screen disappeared, if the lights suddenly went on or off, he could continue. There is an iceberg beneath the tip. The totally inexperienced speaker, on the other hand, is the servant of his script and equipment, is betraying his nervousness by gestures, most of which he is unaware of. He exudes un-confidence – speaking quickly (presumably to get it over with?), quietly (so he won't commit himself?), on one level (because the text has no light or shade). He is reading rather than performing. The professional is performing.

This chapter won't turn the incompetent into a pro but it should help the aspirant to perform better.

And it *is* a performance. Speaking is a performing art. And everything contributes to the performance. Nevertheless it's *your* performance. You must not pretend to be someone else. This may not be the normal you but it's a recognizable you nevertheless. The performance brings out the best in you, maybe an unsuspected you – but not an alien you!

What you will learn the more you watch presenters is that the professional gives a *total* performance. ('Meaning . . . resides in a total act of communication.') The bad presenter, afraid of committing himself, attempts to give a *restricted* performance. He attempts a half-gesture, he reverts to an awkard stance, perhaps hiding his hands in his pockets. He reads his script, looks at the screen – anything to avoid engaging the audience in eye contact. And by avoiding the audience he encourages the audience to avoid him.

The onus *always* is on the transmitter.

The presenter must be *in charge*. From the beginning.

Obvious signs of nerves – a dry voice, a shaking hand, pauses filled with 'um' and 'er' – immediately communicate a sense of unease. An apology will merely confirm it. The obviously nervous speaker makes the audience nervous.

How then to disguise nerves and immediately take charge?

Think positive. You have something to say and the audience wants to hear it. You have two or three minutes with the audience clearly on your side. It is probably sympathetic. You have its respect. You have no reason to believe it is hostile. You can of course make it hostile but at the outset you have a free run.

And small mistakes which you are aware of because you know what should have happened are likely not to be noticed by the audience who don't know.

Remember also you may look only one tenth as bad as you feel.

Particularly if you smile.

And take your time.

The un-confident speaker is the victim of time. The confident speaker establishes his own time. Therefore if you can manage to control your timing in your opening minutes you will create a feeling of confidence in the audience which in turn will create confidence in you. Take your time. It will help you – and the audience. It will need time to size you up. Practise your opening remarks. Build in a pause.

Think of the audience not as a mass but as a bunch of individuals. Focus in your mind upon one. After all if you have followed the advice in **PIT** then you will have been helped in the preparation of the text by Eric. Bring him with you to the hall. You've got to know him. You know what concerns him, where he may have difficulties, what alleviates those problems.

Everything communicates. You must practise control of the total you – voice, intonation, gesture, manner, appearance. The totality is your style. And, as Quintilian reminds us, 'the duty of the orator is to speak in a style fitted to convince'. [4]

You will never convince an audience of anything by boring it. You can bore an audience – even with the most interesting text – by delivering it in a monotone. Monotonous delivery has two ill effects. First, its strict regulatory beat acts hypnotically on the audience, the aural equivalent of counting sheep. Second, the sameness of the delivery transfers to the text itself, so that the emphases, shape, even the argument, are submerged, homo-genized, in a bland uniform utterance.

Variety in the text must become variety in the delivered presentation. The script must be marked for emphases, pauses, pace – light and shade. Presentations are meant to be heard. The voice has to perform the function of punctuation. It has to *express* underlinings, italics, question marks, commas, full stops, a sequence of dots . . . The more the script is an-notated the more the presenter will be in control. Why? Because he combats noise with *variety*. The opposite of monotony.

'The actor's voice', Christopher Turk reminds us, 'is an instrument of great flexibility, continually varying, continually exploring the range of expression.' [5]

The audience's attention span is short. It has continually to be aroused, encouraged. Turk distinguishes six dimensions in which the voice can be manipulated to bring variety – **pause, pace, pitch, tone, volume, intonation.**

Pause

If you've been thinking like a listener and have prepared a script, you'll have incorporated pauses for audience participation. Remember, every presentation has audience participation. If not there is no communication.

Pauses are the valleys which let the listener see the peaks. Pauses should bracket groups of words which relate to a single thought. You may use a pause before a key word for emphasis. You may wish to make a pause in order to breathe. Don't. Make a pause for effect – and then breathe.

Pace

Pace is probably the easiest dimension to vary. Try to establish your normal speaking speed. Practise with a tape recorder and with a colleague. Is the meaning coming through? Now examine the script and see where you should slow down and where speed up.

Slow down for emphasis. Speed up for climax.

There must be conventions. Pace is part of the collection of signals which constitute your code. That code must be understood by the audience (shared meaning). Changing your pace at random will communicate conflicting signals. For example, if you choose to speak slowly at the key sections where you want the audience to remember, you must avoid speaking slowly later simply because you are underrunning on time. Far better to end early than suggest unwanted added significance. Similarly make sure that the pace of delivery matches the subject matter. If you say 'so let's quickly recap', then do that. Don't drag it out.

Don't change pace for the sake of change. Change for a reason. And those reasons must be dictated by the text (and indicated in the script) before you mount the stage. Pace should not be dictated by the pressure of time on the day itself. This means constant practice. Real practice. Not speaking quickly to yourself, in your head, but out loud, at full speaking voice at the appropriate pace and changing the script where appropriate.

Pitch

The golden rule about pitch is – 'lower it'. Most nervous speakers are high-pitched. And most high-pitched speakers are nervous. Conversely a lower-pitched voice suggests confidence. Read your opening section into a tape recorder. Play it back. Then record it at a lower pitch. Compare the effects. Then take a section from the body of the talk and record at high and low pitch. Then try in between, at your normal pitch. Then tape your closing remarks at the three levels. You will probably find that the high-pitched version sounds unnatural, and it is communicating more and different signals than you intended. Your normal pitch, whilst adequate for the body of the talk, may be less appropriate for the opening and closing remarks. But whatever happens you will appreciate that variety is essential and that choices need to be made – and before you begin.

Of course these dimensions are not discrete. A change in pitch coinciding with a change in pace can be very effective. An aside, for example, is best said at a low pitch bracketed by short pauses.

Tone

It's surprising how few presenters change their tone during a speech. Probably they are afraid of 'acting'. And yet in real life they adopt a variety of tones. They can be impassioned, angry, friendly, serious, objective, cheeky, calm, surprised. In the course of twenty minutes' delivery of a well put together presentation it is unlikely that a change of tone isn't suggested. The change can enhance what is being said. For example, if you wish to put across a surprising statistic you could adopt a quizzical tone, raising your voice at the end of the sentence to indicate a questioning disbelief. Similarly if you seriously feel impatient with, say, a piece of government inactivity then do not deliver it in the same calm manner as the bulk of your speech. You should adopt an angry tone of voice and consider raising the pitch, increasing the pace, increasing the volume.

Volume

Volume is a variant but one to be used sparingly. The key consideration is the right degree of volume to fill the filled room. With microphones and amplification the volume of the speaker's own voice may not be that high. Ideally it should be a bit higher than the volume at which you would normally talk. Remember, if actors talked as they normally talk they would not be heard throughout the theatre. What really matters is projection, the ability to throw your voice rather than swallow it. There are useful projection exercises in books on speech training.

Occasional changes in volume can be effective. Increased for emphasis. Reduced for incidental, off-the-cuff comments.

Intonation

Intonation is varied automatically in normal conversation according to the type of remark we utter. The voice rises or falls. It rises when we ask a question, or express indecision, or if we are shy, hesitant or doubtful. On

Arsenal 1 Chelsea...

Derby County 2 Liverpool...

Everton 0 Southampton...

INTONATION POOLS. Who drew?
Who won at home? Who won away?

the other hand, when we make a statement or are being assertive, firm, confident, our voice falls. It almost always falls at the end of a speech to indicate finality.

Intonation also is determined by the stress you wish to put upon one part of a sentence.

Here is a seemingly simple sentence.

One man in this room is lying.

There are in fact no fewer than seven variants in meaning according to which of the seven words you accent. (Try it out.)

Check your own intonation by recording your speech. Have you put the emphasis in the right place? (Is what you *mean* what you thought you were saying?) What happens if you change emphasis?

And while you are listening check for clarity. Better still ask someone else to listen. It is always harder to listen to an unseen voice since the listener can't check the shape or movement of the mouth.

Public speaking is *not* conversation. It may occasionally give the impression of being cosy and friendly, even intimate. But this is always an illusion, the art that hides art. Public speakers *must* enunciate. You must never mumble, run words together, swallow syllables or forget to move your mouth.

*Mirror, mirror, on the wall—
who's the finest orator
of them all?*

You should check your delivery in a mirror. If your friend has a problem understanding your taped voice it may be useful to practise enunciation exercises every day. The more you read aloud (preferably in front of a mirror and near a tape recorder) the better. Try to make each syllable distinct. Check whether you are running words together or clipping words. Each syllable has a right to be heard. Ignore them and you create noise, even change the meaning of your text.

24 In Control of Yourself

In this chapter we examine control of those parts of yourself you may usually have less obvious control of.

Quintilian said 'How much importance a gesture has is manifest enough from the simple reflection that it can signify most things even without words.' [1]

The novice speaker suffers a double handicap. He may gesture unconsciously and he may gesture consciously but ineffectively.

The rule for the beginner is 'if in doubt – out'. Though the correct gesture can heighten the effect of what is said, the risk of ruining that effect is too great to run.

Gestures have to be practised. But, you say, most of us make gestures in normal conversation. Why practise? Because our normal gestures may not be communicating what we intend; because most gestures may not be big enough for an audience; and because gesturing while reading is something we don't do – normally.

Some presenters gesture for one reason only. They don't otherwise know what to do with their hands. The result is nearly always awkward and disturbing. It transmits noise, evidence of a lack of confidence and, perhaps falsely, a lack of control of their subject matter. The answer is not to put one's hands in one's pockets or fold one's arms. My advice is to grasp the lectern lightly and lean forward. This keeps the hands in view and the stance automatically makes the presenter move towards the audience and thus helps establish contact.

As a presenter becomes more confident so he can remove his hands from the lectern. Eventually he becomes so proficient that the lectern becomes merely the resting place for hands between gestures.

Gestures must be definite. There is no such thing as a half-gesture. Gestures are like pregnancy – you can't be partly pregnant. If you point, then point with the full arm outstretched. (But rarely to the audience.) Similarly if you use a pointer make sure it is a straight line extension of your arm.

And don't fiddle with the pointer. Or wave it about. Before you know it your gestures are emphasizing something different from your voice.

...We are poles apart on this issue...

.. maintain the balance of trade...

... I flew over from New York...

...in a wide-bodied jet...

Don't make too many gestures. But do make them consistent. If stretching out your hands is meant to indicate size, don't use the identical gesture to indicate something else or (as is common) nothing at all. Too many presenters gesture for gesture's sake.

I've only one thing to say...   As God's my judge...   The roof is going to fall in...   The nicotine will tell you I'm a heavy smoker...

Make sure your gestures mean one thing

Gestures must be *perfectly* timed. If they are used to accompany text then invariably the gesture must just precede the spoken word. 'We are going (*point*) forward.' Not 'We are going forward (*point*).'

Actions may speak louder than words. But the wrong gestures will speak the wrong words.

Leaving the lectern, walking across the stage, picking up a glass of water or a prop, turning to the screen . . . each of these movements must be definitely done – and with a purpose. It is not done for your own convenience (i.e. because you are tired of where you are standing) but for the audience's benefit. For example, you move to the front of the stage in order to enlist the help of a volunteer from the audience, or you pick up a prop, not to have something to fiddle with and calm your nerves, but because you are about to demonstrate something to the audience which will increase their understanding of your argument.

Inexperienced speakers seem to believe that any sort of movement indicates confidence and ease of manner. The reverse is the case.

Unless the presenter is aware of the unhelpful effect he is creating it is difficult to convince him of the need to control his gestures. A videotaped session is helpful. It will reveal where the unstructured conscious gestures ('I see what you mean') and the unconscious mannerisms ('Good lord, I didn't know I did *that!*') undermine his message.

All speakers have physical mannerisms. The professional keeps most in check and harnesses the rest. The novice, particularly if nervous, rubs his face, strokes his neck or moustache, tilts his head, brushes his hair with his hand or plays with any object on the table or lectern in front of him. Very often he puts his hands in front of his mouth. This communicates a desire to hide and renders the speaker inaudible.

At all costs keep your hands away from your face.

Do not wipe your forehead.
Do not clench your fists.
Do not scratch – anything!

Never speak with your hands behind your back or in your pockets. Try to avoid holding your hands, arms stretched, level with your pelvis. Don't fold your arms. Don't sway back and forth. And if and when you leave the lectern or whatever fixed position, don't put your hands on your hips and pace up and down in front of the audience. As the authors of *The Business Guide to Effective Speaking* point out, this 'gives the audience the feeling it's being interrogated. (We've found [this] to be the favourite position of the police and the military.)' [2]

Body language is potent. The speaker's position relative to the audience will communicate degree of identification. Proximity, angle, bodily contact . . . these aspects of nonverbal communication will all transmit messages quite as important as the text. Argyle distinguishes two categories of nonverbal aspects of speech – prosodic and paralinguistic signals.[3] The prosodic are the patterns of pitch and stress, the pauses and timing. These he says affect the meaning and are 'true parts of verbal utterance'. Conversely the paralinguistic signals are 'emotions expressed by the *tone of voice* . . . voice quality, speech errors, emotional state' (my italics). A fast and breathy delivery denotes anxiety. The use of an accent may convey group membership.

As we have quoted, 'meaning . . . resides in the total act of communication.' And not all body language is unconscious. Nor is all unconscious body language counterproductive. There is a need to practise and monitor one's progress until the conscious gestures are perfected, the unconscious restricted and harnessed.

With nonverbal communication (NVC) the viewer is in charge. He can decide what to believe. He may indeed regard NVC as the real message and the presentation as noise. The speaker's opening remark 'I am happy to be here' may be totally undermined by a nervous tic. On the other hand, a speaker sharing a joke from the hall may well communicate the idea that he *is* happy to be here.

Whereas verbal communication (and accompanying visuals) is used to convey information, NVC 'is used to manage the immediate social relationship'.[4] As Abercrombie says, 'We speak with our vocal organs, but we communicate with our whole body.' [5]

Including our dress. The rule is simple. Dress for sound – not noise. Does the style help you communicate (as Quintilian said)? Or does unkempt hair distract the audience, or you, so that you try to keep it in place and thereby distract the audience even further? Does your tie or jewellery shout? (Note that it's no accident that the word for garish clothes is 'loud' – too much

noise.) On the other hand, you should not make yourself invisible. Most of most speakers is already invisible – much less than the top half can be seen over a lectern. A tie fading into a same-coloured shirt and/or suit, or a blouse under a same-coloured jacket, can cause the speaker to retreat even further. I opt for a bow tie since all of it can be seen by the audience.

Avoid drawing attention to your dress, e.g. adjusting a scarf or tie, pulling out a handkerchief, pulling down a cuff. This communicates to the audience that you are deliberately trying to achieve an effect.

There are various other forms of noise – verbal mannerisms, for example. Most of us use certain phrases – 'if you like', 'you know', 'in point of fact', 'it should be said', or foreign tag lines, idiosyncratic sentence constructions, etc. These can be spotted early enough in the written text. In the more spontaneous form of delivery, however, you may not realize their frequency. The audience will soon notice the oft-repeated phrase or gesture.

It will become a mannerism the audience waits for – at the expense of the subject matter. I've known audiences count the incidence of particular mannerisms.

There are also vocal mannerisms. 'Talking downwards to the floor or table, turning away, dropping the pitch and diminishing the volume to fade out at the end of sentences – these are common ones', says John May.[6] He also cites those 'semi-animal mannerisms – grunts, sighs, erm-ahs, nervous coughs, and unnecessary laughs'. These are also known as pause-fillers. They are a sign of a less than confident speaker. The confident speaker will not fill the pause because he can hold the audience's attention. And even when the pause is caused by a momentary loss for words the professional knows (a) he will find them, and (b) the short silence will arouse expectation. Ums and ers merely create noise.

25 Holding the Audience

We move now from control of self to control of the audience. Not, of course, that the two are unrelated. You will exert little control of the audience if you aren't in charge of yourself. What we concentrate on in this section, though, is the *relationship* between transmitter and receiver. And the need for the first to understand the second.

The good presenter can hold an audience. No presenter can hold an audience against its will.

Speakers fail when they lose themselves in their presentation and become obsessed with their argument to the exclusion of those to whom it is addressed. Even the best put together presentation can fail if the presenter merely reads his script, no matter how passionately, without establishing eye contact, inviting a reaction, pausing – whether for effect or relief – in other words without recognizing and appreciating not simply the audience's presence but its vital contribution to the presentation.

Think like the listener and you will remember the attention curve. You have his attention at the outset – as a free gift. Use that time. Don't abuse it. Attention drops after about ten minutes. Now you have to build upon the good work of your opening. Your script should contain new material, but your performance too needs to be refreshed – by gesture, pause, question, demonstration, change of pace, change of intonation, a surprise slide, etc.

But – it goes without saying – these devices, whilst refreshing, must also *reinforce* your argument. They must play to your *point*. It is very easy to *divert* an audience, to entertain it with a succession of anecdotes, jokes, illustrations. Your job is persuasion, not diversion. Everything must be related to the subject of your argument, to its point. And the style must suit.

Attention will automatically climb towards the end. If your presentation has been single-minded then your conclusion, the key section for the audience to remember, will be seen to be a natural summation and reinforcement of all that has gone before. On the other hand, if your central section is a series of *divertissements* then the audience may be puzzled by your conclusion.

Your performance must aid your argument – and be appropriate to it. If it is not appropriate it creates noise and detracts from your argument.

Let's remind ourselves of the three forms of noise which can diminish our signal.

They are **code** (or language) noise, **channel** noise and **psychological** noise.

Some of the *code* noise has been eliminated in the preparation of the text. By the time it becomes a script the language should be clear for a listener. Difficult thought processes will have been eased out. A long complex sentence will have become a series of interlinked short ones. Difficult words will have been replaced, explained or illustrated. We will have replaced jargon with user-friendly terms (if you'll excuse the jargon). We will have eliminated any possible misinterpretation by speaking the text to a colleague.

However, that is not the end of possible code noise. Pronunciation or accent or a speech defect may cause misunderstanding. Roy Jenkins on the radio made 'breakthrough' sound like 'grapefruit'. And even the most seemingly harmless word or term in the text may cause problems to an audience not as familiar with your subject as you or a colleague. Remember the term 'debtor nations' which may make a lay listener wonder what explosions have to do with banking.

There is, of course, a totally different form of code noise in performance. It is the code you choose to adopt with regard to your material and equipment. As we've seen it's essential that the use of type-sizes, capitals and lower case letters is consistent; that the relationship between you and your screen, or the parts played by the overhead projector and a slide projector, are understood by the audience. Unless you establish your code at the outset these speaker aids may become barriers to communication.

Channel noise, of course, is the most potentially damaging form during actual presentation. Rehearsal is crucial. Preparation helps. So does assuming the worst. The bulb that blows (always bring a spare). The sound system that packs up in the coffee break – or picks up a passing radio cab. The slide that jams. The upside-down slide (the one you replaced at the last minute, remember?). The inadequate lighting. The coffee cups. The meeting in the room next door. The heating. The ventilation. And more, which we'll meet in a future chapter.

Finally, *psychological* noise. This is no longer a question of the listener not hearing or not understanding but of not accepting what is heard. He may be out of sympathy with the message or the presenter or the occasion or indeed out of sorts with himself. He could be daydreaming (don't we all at conferences?) or worried about what's going on at the office.

Whatever the cause, he is not involved. Your job is to involve him – or fail in the attempt.

And you must involve him at the beginning. Do not assume that because attention comes as a free gift you don't need to engage the audience's interest. Attention and interest are different things. A famous traditional model of the advertising process is known as AIDA –

Attention
Interest
Desire
Action

These are the four stages a reader is meant to go through from first catching sight of a press ad to buying the product. It is somewhat simplistic but it gets its priorities right – and it serves to distinguish four entirely separate emotions.

Attention is not interest.

The first you may be given. The second you have to earn. As you do the third and fourth – if you want the audience to desire your product, your message, and go out and *do* something.

You have to make contact with the audience. Friendly contact. Smile. (It may be the last thing you feel capable of or justified in doing but the response of the audience may encourage you and bring justification.) Most of the audience is far from hostile. A smile is a message. It says you're pleased to see them or that you know that they know what you're going through. It says that you like them.

But make sure it's a big smile. Overdo it. A weak, nervous grin will produce a negative effect. And half-gestures do not exist. What may appear overacting to you will appear quite normal to the audience. And if it makes you happier smile at the man or the woman in the back row.

A big smile and quick contact with the audience says you're in charge.

Get control straight away – and never lose it!

Look at the audience. All of it. That does not mean each and every member. But each and every section.

If possible start with the lights up. When you become proficient stand away from the lectern for your introduction. Try always to use a neck mike for greater freedom. Address your first words as close to the audience as possible. You could try (later) starting to speak from your seat or the front row as you rise. In other words do whatever you can not to distance yourself from the audience. And do not use the lectern as a fortress.

As you look at the audience look for a friendly face. If you've done your homework you'll know something about the composition of the audience. You may have been talking to a few of them prior to your presentation.

Do *not*, though, fix your gaze on one person throughout. Do not fix your gaze on *anything* throughout.

Certainly not the screen – and especially when there's nothing on it! And certainly not your script, though that's the spot where your gaze will rest longest. Remember, a good presenter will *refer* to his script rather than read it.

If you begin with a joke (and it should be relevant, not gratuitous) tell all of it out front. Your eyes must never leave the audience.

And if you can set the scene for your presentation similarly – out front – so much the better. It immediately communicates that you're in control of your subject. And that will enable you to be in control of your audience.

The first few minutes are vital. Use them to move from attention to interest. Use them to learn.

Tyrone Guthrie, the drama producer, used to teach his actors to imagine

Imagine you are throwing a rope to the audience

that they were throwing a rope to the audience. The audience had to catch it. And never let go. Tension had to be maintained throughout the play. But the audience's hold would depend upon the actor's performance.

In the first few minutes of a presentation (or a simple after-dinner speech) you are throwing out your rope. Has it been caught? How taut is it?

The more the presenter learns, the more feedback he receives, the more able is he to perfect his delivery. The first thing he learns, of course, is whether there is an audience there at all! The joke may fall flat. A reference may not be appreciated. There is no feedback.

Don't panic. It happens to the professional speaker, to the experienced comic. The audience may be shy, puzzled, cautious. Explain what you are doing – establishing contact. Don't apologize. Settle upon one of your friendly faces. Ask a question.

'Anybody here speak English?' You'll get a smile. Maybe a laugh. 'Thank you.'

Your first few minutes are research. The stand-up comic knows this. He can soon tell how fast his audience is, how much allowance he has to make for understanding, whether he and the audience are on the same wavelength, how much he has to adjust. He may have to change some of his material.

It's the same with the presenter.

Maintain eye contact. Only by looking at the audience can you gauge interest, detect boredom or sense difficulty in comprehension.

Feedback is there. You can tell whether people believe you, whether they are surprised, whether they agree, are puzzled, annoyed or indifferent.

Your first few minutes are research

A presentation is half of a dialogue. It is meaningless without reference to, and acknowledgement of, the receiver. It is ludicrous to elicit feedback (whether intentionally or not) and not act upon it.

This does not mean stopping every moment to rewrite your speech or answer an implied question. It does mean an occasional pause to check comprehension, a repetition of a key fact, maybe, or an ad-lib to put the passage you have reached into context. (A map of the course on permanent display is a useful prop to refer to at this juncture.)

The more you can do to avoid an adversarial atmosphere the better. You do not persuade people to your point of view by first making enemies of them. If you can involve your audience in the presentation itself you can demonstrate in a small way your identification with their interest.

You can ask for a volunteer (maybe before you begin) in order to demonstrate a point – or merely to help you with the equipment.

You can ask questions of the audience.

It's a risk, of course. I once asked an audience what certain advertisements had in common. An anti-advertising art teacher in the audience shouted 'debasement'. To which I replied, 'No sir, de basement is downstairs, dis is de ground floor.' Which made it fifteen all.

But you can avoid direct vocal response by asking for a show of hands. 'How many of you agree with this statement?'

A show of hands is a simple but most effective form of participation. It revives interest, especially if the lighting level changes. It provides exercise. It is entirely spontaneous – a touch of drama. And it involves every member of the audience – without embarrassing any of them. Participation can backfire if a member of the audience is felt to be intimidated.

Of course the person most likely to feel intimidated (justifiably or not) is the presenter. Intimidated by the inanimate equipment – or the animate audience. He may take personally the fidgeting in the front row, the yawn, the rustling of papers, the reading of newspapers, the conversation in the third row, the silent but conspicuous departure of a delegate.

As one old speaker's joke put it, 'I get concerned when a member of the audience looks as his watch. But when he picks it up, puts it to his ear, and shakes it, I get *worried*.'

This is a theme I would very much like to develop

...on some future occasion

A presenter is right to take those signs personally. They *are* items of feedback, evidence perhaps of uninterest or disagreement. But not always. People do leave because they have other engagements. Try not to draw attention to them. Refrain from saying goodbye. But if they apologize then acknowledge. Do not scold them.

If people talk in the audience you may need to lower your voice so that their conversation becomes proportionately louder, a technique advocated by A. L. Kirkpatrick.[1] This has the effect of embarrassing them and eliciting the support of the rest of the audience. Alternatively you could pause to let them finish. Again, try not to engage them in an argument. The more proficient you become the more capable you will be of dealing with talkers, perhaps with a suitable one-liner.

Hecklers are another matter. Heckling is always deliberate. But it is also a form of feedback, hostile admittedly. The rule here is never play away. Do not adopt the heckler's tactics. Hear him out the first time. Answer him. If he continues dismiss him – if possible with a polite put-down. If he persists, with an impolite one.

This is the toughest test of your audience control. But if you have established contact at the outset; turned attention into interest; maintained control through textural and performance variation; used your antennae to detect feedback and your imagination to respond to it; then you will have won over the audience. And with them on your side a heckler has no chance.

26 Presenter and Equipment

It can't be said too often. *You* are in charge, and the more you rehearse the more in charge.

Equipment and material are your servants not your masters. If you don't need them don't use them. But if you do need them (and that is almost certainly the case) then make sure you know how to.

And this is old Fred, who projected your slides

Sorry about the cock-up, squire

To turn up at a conference with a box of assorted slides, unnumbered, with no blanks and no marked script is an offence to the organizers. To proceed to the stage with no rehearsal and bellow orders and expletives is an offence to the crew. The resulting performance is an offence to the audience.

Deafening noise switches the audience off.

Less intense noise merely distracts. Though that can damage your presentation and frustrate your intention.

Never share a screen, says the old Hollywood adage, with a baby or an animal. Or, we could add, with a slide or film projector. Unless, that is, you are seen to be in charge of it. Lurking there unused or projecting an introductory slide which has outrun its purpose and outworn its welcome, the projector can only distract. The visual aid becomes noise.

A presentation is show business. The audience believes that everything on the stage is there for a purpose, that it is part of the presentation. Indeed why shouldn't the audience believe that? It gives the organizers and you the credit for being professional. Presumably if you didn't want something to be shown or used then you would not leave it in full view of the audience.

A presentation is showbusiness

You must ask yourself – at the rehearsal ideally but on the day if necessary – what the stage, the set, the props, the equipment, the totality is saying. Meaning, remember, exists in the totality of the communication.

In a fascinating study of communication in the theatre, Keir Elam discusses the work of the Prague school of structuralist critics.[1] Until 1981, he says, 'the descriptive science of the drama and theatrical performances had made little substantial progress since its Aristotelian origin'.[2] The Prague school made it less exclusively the property of literary critics and examined the total effect of communication in performance. The text no longer automatically dominated. It had to 'take its place in the system of systems making up the total dramatic representation'.[3]

The stage, he says, 'radically transforms all objects and bodies defined within it'.[4] They 'acquire special features, qualities and attributes that they do not have in real life'.[5]

Is a presentation 'real life'? I would suggest not. We have already discussed the artificiality of the exercise. The simplest set in the smallest room is no less theatrical given the fact of the performance than the ready-made 'stage' of the medieval morality play.

One person standing up in front of others at an agreed time and place, being afforded attention and inviting participation, is a theatrical event.

Text is not the 'total dramatic representation'. Nor indeed is the delivery. Everything on that 'stage' communicates. Or, to quote Jiri Veltrusky of the Prague school,

All that is on the stage is a sign.[6]

'The audience starts', says Elam, 'with the assumption that every detail is an intentional sign.' [7] Again, why not? Think how we react as an audience.

The covered flipchart is a sign that the presenter has something to show us. The fact that it was left over from a previous presentation begins to dawn only some way through the presentation. The way the chairs are arranged on the dais signifies a discussion. We wonder when that will happen. Immediately after the presenter's formal talk, i.e. as part of the total presentation? In which case who will join him? Maybe somebody from the audience? Me maybe?! Or perhaps it's there for the *next* session, this afternoon? The chairman has remained seated on stage. He's beneath the screen. That means there won't be any slides because he won't be able to see them from there. We'd see them all right. Presumably he's going to join in? On the small table next to the overhead projector there are acetates and a pen. The presenter will use those. Or maybe the chairman later, or during the show to help the speaker. There's a second lectern with a light on it. That signifies a second presenter.

Everything communicates.

You must ensure that unnecessary signals are not being transmitted.

Don't allow anything to remain on the stage which you don't need and which can be moved. Even if you may need it *during* the presentation, see if it's possible to bring it on, or reveal it by a change of lighting, exactly when it is needed. Not only will this eliminate noise, it will revive attention rather than act as a distraction.

And when you use a visual aid remember the triangle – you, the audience and the screen (or whatever). Do not come between the audience and the screen. Do not turn your back on the audience.

If you use a video playback machine, thoroughly familiarize yourself with the controls. Better still, get help. Practise with one of the crew. It is too easy on the day to hit the wrong button or press rewind for too long. One advantage of employing an operator is that it avoids the necessity of having the machine on the platform.

Rehearsal is vital. Particularly if you wish to stop and start. This demands blank leader between the items of tape, careful checking of the numbers on the meter and periodic checking of the rewind when the machine stops. Pause buttons can be used but not when an image is projected. The skilful operator will run on to a blank leader, check the number just prior to the next item, *then* press the pause button and release it upon your cue.

Can you see now why you shouldn't attempt all this yourself?

Whatever you use – video playback machine, film or slide projector – do not point across your body to the screen. Make sure the lectern is angled inwards, that you can see the screen out of the corner of your nearer eye and that you point (if and when necessary) to the screen with *that* arm. If you use a pointer don't fidget with it. Don't fidget with anything!

Make sure you have the appropriate slide buttons and switches easily to hand – and clearly marked. Know the forward from the reverse button. If

Can anyone tell
me where the
switch is?

some of the controls are not being used cover them with sticky tape. Keep the remote control switch loosely attached to the lectern – and away from other wires (e.g. neck mike). Modern remote controls dispense with wires anyway.

If you aren't in control of your equipment you may not immediately lose your audience, but you may lose confidence, which will eventually amount to the same thing. You will lose your sense of timing.

Timing is difficult even without visual aids. Visual aids make it more so since you now have to co-ordinate the visual aid with the spoken voice, the slide button with your vocal chord.

The crew can press your button for you if you provide a marked script – and keep to it. But this takes control out of your hands. It probably prevents you from ad-libbing. If you do intend to depart from the script then it is crucial that you warn the crew and that you nonetheless stick to the cue words.

Learn how long the gap is between pressing the button and the appearance of the slide. Systems vary. Don't bring a slide on too soon. Err, if you must, on the side of later rather than sooner. But aim for perfect synchronisation. This demands practice. Synchronisation does not entail pressing the button on the word you want to screen but a word or two before. Be careful, therefore, that you do not gesture for emphasis with the hand holding the remote control.

Your presentation may be complex. It may employ two screens and anything from three to nine projectors. There is no way you can operate that yourself. Indeed at that level of sophistication it's doubtful if you'll be needed anyway – live, that is. You'll be on a video or relegated to a voice-over.

However, you may be faced with the choice of single or twin carousel. The former is a straightforward 'clunk-clunk' progression of slides with a microsecond of blank between. The latter is a smooth fade-out/fade-in progression so that one slide replaces another uninterruptedly in the manner of a cinema dissolve.

Though the latter is more sophisticated it is not always the more appropriate. It necessitates a careful alternate arrangement of slides in two carousel magazines. Adjustments are complicated. And reversing is virtually impossible. The choice depends largely upon the purpose of the presentation. The smooth show is enhanced by dissolves. The participative and spontaneous show is inhibited by it.

My usual preference is 'clunk-clunk'. What it lacks in elegance it makes up for in *contact*. I feel more at ease with my material and more capable of getting at it if and when necessary.

A single magazine presentation is of course far easier to rehearse with. You can familiarize yourself not only with the content but with the impression it will make. Whereas if you rehearse with single magazine and project with a twin carousel you may be surprised by the pace and atmosphere of the occasion. Also it is quite common for rehearsals to take place the day before with single magazine, only to change to the more expensive set-up (hired for the real occasion) on the day itself.

A word about the conclusion. The final slide. What is it? How long is it up? Who pushes the button? Too few presenters plan the ending of their presentations.

Make sure there is a blank immediately after your last slide – even if your last slide is a blank. You may be tempted to press the button once too often and reveal a screen full of white light.

Envisage the set as you finish. If you're to remain there to answer questions what is the audience looking at? Have you created a mess or have you left a suitable *aide-mémoire* in full view on which the audience can concentrate and so remember your point?

Nothing says you are in control as much as your exit. Particularly to deserved applause.

27 Drama

There is one good reason for thinking of a presentation as drama. Drama is meant to be *performed*. John Whiting, in his book *The Art of the Dramatist*, says of the playwright, 'his play would be no play if it remained words on paper'.[1]

Too many presentations read better than they sound. They remain words on paper. This is due partly to the wrong use of language (and possibly to the use of the wrong language), i.e. not structuring for speech. It is due also to the writer's lack of sensitivity to the occasion of performance.

Both of these faults result from a failure to appreciate the importance of *time*. As we have noted time is little problem for the reader. He can go back. Time is a severe constraint, however, for the listener – and therefore the writer, whether of a presentation or a play, combats the passage of time by carefully structuring his sentences and relating one to another. But this skill by itself won't make the performance 'dramatic'. The presentation may be understood perfectly but it won't catch fire unless first, the writer has planned the development, not simply of his argument but of his action; and second, the presenter can deliver.

We are talking about a sense of timing. No text or performance succeeds without it.

'The basic, the unalterable factor of drama', says Whiting, 'is the moment "when"; the moment of happening which is contained in the action . . . In other words, the dramatist must create what is done and *when*, and not only the words to be spoken.' [2]

That goes too for the writer of a presentation. He must create his work in *time*. He must timetable the parts. Time is the dimension he works in. Not the spatial printed page. He, as Whiting suggests, must be concerned above all not simply with what is said or how it is said but also *when* it is said.

In scripting a presentation he has to make his major points at moments of most impact. He has to arrange his argument to achieve a climax. There may be a succession of mini climaxes culminating in a major one, say, five-sixths of the way through the presentation. He knows too that climaxing early will mean less impact and a consequent loss of interest for the audience. The same considerations apply, of course, to the presenter during the presentation. Too much 'drama' in his performance early on may unbalance the presentation. A piece of 'theatre' may help him gain the audience's attention. But it may be the equivalent of wasting a trump card. Later on a similar piece of theatre, relevant to his point, would serve to *maintain the audience's interest.*

The presenter is taking the audience through an argument through time.

A presentation *is* theatre. There is a stage. There is an audience. There is a sense of performance.

The writer/presenter must envisage the performance as he writes. If he shuts himself away in the manuscript page he will end up with a text read aloud. If he thinks of a live audience in a large room, and of the thirty or so minutes' performance, and listens to the listener in the chair opposite, he will end up with not just a spoken script but a dramatic presentation.

And that means *live*. No two performances are identical. There is a feeling of 'being there', as it happens. And of wondering what will happen – how will it end? The very fact which makes the presenter nervous is the fact which gives the presenter such potential power – immediacy. It takes place in real time. There's no going back. And it may all go wrong.

But that's a prime ingredient of drama. No tension, no drama.

The drama, of course, must exist in the writing. It can't be discursive. It must not move down a succession of side roads. It must take the audience forward.

But if the writer has to create tension he is in turn helped by the tension provided by the constraints which he is under. The artist's job is to exploit his limitations. He welcomes discipline. It is a creative necessity. The painter demands the frame, the poet the sonnet form. For the dramatist the conventions of the stage.

As we have seen already, the writer of the presentation enjoys three disciplines. They happen to be the three rules of drama originated by

Aristotle and codified by the neo-classical critics of the seventeenth century.

(And that's not as fanciful as it sounds.) The three unities are those of place, of time and of action.

The presentation occurs in one place. There is no change of set. The presenter stays on the stage. He may use the screen to take the audience to other places. He may wander from his podium. But the presentation has only one focal point – where the presenter chooses to present.

The presentation occurs in real time. Thirty minutes equals thirty minutes. Classical tragedy did not attempt to portray the whole history of the character. Instead it chose to present the story at *the closing stages*. The action unfolding took place in the time it took to tell. Preceding events were referred to by the characters or the chorus but not shown.

A presentation which endeavours to tell too much, similarly, lacks focus. Unity of action concerns one *story line*. No subplots. There simply is no time for a subplot.

These three unities – place, time, action – assist the presenter. They improve the chances of the presentation being dramatic. They do not, of course, guarantee it. Drama is more than constraints just as a painting is more than a frame.

Drama is about *a character in a situation*. The character has to be recognizably human. His behaviour has to be understood. As does the situation. Otherwise the audience cannot relate. The situation affects the character. The character affects the situation: indeed, he may have caused it.

The interaction of character and situation *is* the drama. How will the tension be resolved? In laughter (comedy) or tears (tragedy)?

Now this may seem a long way from your approaching presentation on the marketing of a new piece of software. But is it?

A business presentation, we established at the outset, is concerned with persuasion. As a presenter you are trying to move the audience to your point of view. Persuasion necessitates the movement of an audience's attitude. It can move from scepticism to open-mindedness, from uninterest to interest, from neutrality to commitment.

The audience at a drama is not asked to be so directly involved. It is an observer. What is observed is the development of a character as the result of its encounter with a situation. With luck and good writing the audience identifies with the character.

At a presentation the audience may well *be* the character. The future of the company, say, will be affected by the outcome of the launch. The drama played out in the presentation is (in the current jargon) a scenario in which they will take part.

Drama is about *development*.

This is where we are. This is about to happen to us (is already happening). How do we react? How do we overcome it? How do we turn it to our advantage? Climax – proposed course of action – outcome.

A presentation is about development, if only of an argument. Well structured and well performed, it should involve the audience in wanting to know how the situation is resolved and what happens to the main character – i.e. itself. The main character in a presentation is your audience.

The main character is your audience

Remember the target response. What do you want the members of the audience to think, believe, feel, do as a result of the presentation?

Development. The presentation we discussed in Chapter 8 is an example. The audience was addressed as an advertising jury. It was shown a selection of commercials and asked to judge. After the presentation, on the pretext of the score sheets being lost, they were asked to judge again. The marks were compared.

Development. A character in a play, no matter how apparently static or unconversational the piece, is never the identical character at its conclusion. Something has happened to him. In Greek drama something traumatic. Peripeteia, Aristotle called it - reversal of fortune. Things ain't what they used to be. And will never be the same again. Isn't that - in your own small way - what you wish to achieve with your presentation?

And how is the audience to appreciate this? By a rational analysis of the argument, a calm contemplation of the facts and figures a day or two later? That will certainly help, just as a printed hand-out for subsequent perusal will buttress your presentation.

But presentation is live. Presentation is drama. And the point of your presentation calls for a dramatic effect.

Aristotle had a word for this too. Anagnorisis - discovery. Call it a moment of truth. The moment Oedipus discovers the truth about his father.

Every presentation must have a moment of truth. And it must be related to the point you wish to get across above all others.

Can this be made 'theatrical'?

If the following day your audience could remember only ten seconds of your presentation, how would you fill them? Ideally with a *coup de théâtre* which illuminates your point. There may be lots of opportunities for fireworks throughout your presentation but unless they play to your main point be careful lest they overwhelm it.

The re-marking of the scoresheets in the advertising judging is a *coup de théâtre*.

Here's another.

I give a presentation on the subject of branding; the importance of establishing the identity of the advertiser in an advertisement. About one third of the way into the presentation I project a slide. It is a question: Is brand evident?' 'You must ask that question of any and every advertisement. Of any and every piece of display material. Of any and every piece of commercial communication done in that brand's name. Is brand evident? Ask it of these current advertisements.'

I then screen a series of ads – on slide and on video. At the end I repeat the question. 'Is brand evident?' And then add, almost as an aside, 'Oh by the way, that's also an anagram . . .'.

This will lose me almost a fifth of the audience, crossword enthusiasts mostly, who start rearranging the letters . . .

At the presentation's end I show the slide again. 'Is brand evident? By the way, did anybody solve the anagram? Hands up.'

I point to the first respondent.

'David Bernstein', the respondent says.

'Correct', I reply. 'Here's your prize.' I hand out a copy of my book on advertising. 'That's what I mean by identity.'

A gimmick? Yes. But relevant. And if that's all the audience remember then, since it is the *point* of the presentation, it will remember much more.

Timing, of course, is important. In that example, although the theme (branding) was established at the beginning, the *point* (expressed in the question 'Is brand evident?') was introduced a third of the way in. It was repeated approximately a third of the way from the end when the anagram question was posed. The *coup de théâtre* happened at the conclusion. The point was made.

This is Whiting's 'basic unalterable factor of drama . . . the moment when, the moment of happening which is contained in the action'.

There is incipient drama in every subject. We just have to find it. There are always means of involving the audience, of surprising them.

But be careful of the gimmick for its own sake. Copywriter David Abbott addressing an audience of young advertising people drew a picture of a man upside down. 'That will get you attention', he said. 'But what for?'

He then drew money falling from the man's pockets and added, 'But if

Be careful....

of the gimmick for its own sake

you're selling a new form of trouser pocket which safeguards against coins falling out . . . the picture is more than a gimmick.'

A gimmick will gain attention. A relevant gimmick will maintain interest.

You need to remember the attention curve. Change what Antony Jay calls the 'texture' of the presentation, i.e. the means of communicating to the audience. A switch from slide to overhead, from speech to recorded sound, from semi-darkness to full light; a change in pace or volume or pitch; the introduction of a live three-dimensional object ... all these are legitimate tricks of the theatre.

Another is the mistake. A colleague, Peter Townsend, always builds in a mistake. (Some presenters don't need to!) For example, bring on an acetate out of sequence, correct yourself and tell the audience it will see it later. This wakes up the audience, maybe gains sympathy and certainly imprints the image on its mind. We always pay greater attention to those things we're not supposed to see. Letters addressed to other people are irresistible.

A conjuror starts a trick. It doesn't work. He does something else. Later in the act he tries the first trick again. It works.

Another technique is to show a slide apparently the wrong way round. You correct it and it communicates something else. You then revert to the original image and make sense of it.

Of course the chosen illustration or question is key. The rule by now should be plain. Theatrical effects must be relevant to, if possible must express, your point.

If character and situation are two elements of drama, the third is style. Style is another unity. It exists in the writing and is expressed in the performance. As the *Encyclopaedia Britannica* reminds us, 'a play's style controls the kind of gesture and movement of the actor as well as his tone of speech, its pace and inflexion. In this way the attitude of the audience is prepared also . . . Drama is a conventional game, and spectators cannot participate if the rules are constantly broken.' [3]

If you make a theatrical effect be sure it's from the right play. There is no reason not to dress up. The presenter himself, after all, is the most important of his visual aids.

You could put on headgear. The choice is comprehensive: flat cap, trilby, bowler, bonnet, wedding veil, fire department tin hat, mortar board, page boy, top hat, crash helmet, busby, etc., etc.

Your tie or your earrings could light up.

You could put on a wig.

So much for my warm-up joke. Now if you'll bear with me for just a moment...

Even more bizarre, you could *remove* your wig.

But what are you saying? And is it germane to your point?

You could remove your jacket to reveal a message on your shirt or blouse.

You could step from behind the lectern to reveal a bottom half consisting of football shorts and boots or a kilt complete with sporran.

You are bounded by two things only: your imagination – and relevance.

Do not confuse theatrical effects with drama. Such tricks may be justified in terms of reviving the audience's attention but unless they maintain its interest in your point they are not truly dramatic.

For the drama of your presentation resides inherently in the writing. Not just what is said, not just how it's said – but *when*.

28 Humour

You've witnessed it. The nervous speaker rises. A wan smile. A nod to acknowledge the applause. He clears his throat. He thanks the chairperson for the introduction.

And then – the statutory joke. He tells it not because he enjoys telling jokes or because he normally tells jokes. He tells it for two other reasons: he believes the audience expects it and that it will ease his way into the audience's heart and therefore mind.

The joke doesn't work, and is greeted with a few polite noises masquerading as laughs. He turns to his text and begins to read, saying or conveying 'now, to be serious'.

Performances like this give humour a bad name. Whereas it is perfectly legitimate to use humour as a means of getting to know your audience and quickly establishing a rapport, it is a cheap trick to employ it as a sop or a device to win support.

And if the joke doesn't raise a laugh the speaker is worse off than before. Lack of the appropriate response may be due to one of two factors: the material or the telling. The joke may be old, unfunny or inappropriate. This reveals that the speaker has not done his homework on the audience. A joke does not have to be off colour or sectionalist to insult an audience. Poor or threadbare material can just as easily insult its intelligence.

If the joke is badly told another signal is being transmitted. And that, as we shall see in a moment, is a *warning* signal.

So – am I against humour? The reverse. I am against its misuse. It needs careful handling. If I may quote the writer I know best on the subject of humour in advertising ...

> A joke is high explosive. It is a hand grenade. It could win you a street fight; it could also go off in your own hand. Better maybe to leave it alone. Humour is subjective. Some people get a joke which others do not. Moreoever, a joke often doesn't misfire, it backfires. Irony which is not appreciated as such is self-destructive.[1]

The same considerations apply to humour in a presentation. People may remember the joke and forget the product (message). But is this a criticism of humour or of bad presentation? The joke is not relevant or it overwhelms the message.

Humour is high profile. There is no hiding place. It demands an instant and vocal response. Immediate success. Or failure. No wonder people are scared of it. In advertising if you make an error humour increases its visibility. Humour amplifies your mistakes.

Saying something funny in a speech is the verbal equivalent of putting a coupon in the advertisement. If nobody cuts it out and returns it the whole advertisement has not worked – not simply the coupon. If there had been no coupon who would have known?

But the fact that humour is high explosive is reason to use it with care – not an excuse to avoid its use altogether.

Let's examine a few other criticisms before turning to some of humour's benefits for the presenter.

'I may not tell the right joke'

A risk admittedly. However, if you do your homework and learn about the audience you are likely to be near its wavelength. If you can mingle with the audience prior to your presentation you could even try out your quip or anecdote on one or two of them. Don't warn them beforehand of your intention of telling it later but, if the response is good, then inform them that you're thinking of telling it in your talk. What do they think? You now have two confidants in your audience.

Obviously, you can make life easier for yourself by having more than one joke.

'I am not a comedian'

Of course not. Your job is not to tell jokes. You are a presenter. At best you could only be an amateur comedian. Too many jokes and the audience will begin to wonder what you are hiding. When will you get to the point?

"I am not a comedian..."

No – you are not a comedian. Nor should you regard your presentation as a text periodically pitted by gags.

Indeed the less you think of jokes as additional and random optional extras and the more you think of humour as an integral texture variant (in Antony Jay's phrase) the happier you will be and the better your presentation.

'I can't tell jokes'

Not everybody can tell jokes. Not everybody can present.

But the two talents are closely linked. I would go so far as to assert that the bad joke teller is a bad presenter.

Hence the warning signal I mentioned earlier. If the speaker tells a joke badly then probably the presentation will fall flat.

Jokes demand timing. For a joke to work the structure of the story has to be meticulously arranged. The elements have to be fitted together. There is only one correct order. (You have probably met the bad joke teller who stops towards the end of the story and says something like 'oh, I forgot to tell you the parrot was blindfolded'.)

In relating the joke the teller has to take the listener along every step of the way, has to elicit response.

Unless you put it together and put it across you can neither present nor tell a joke.

'I won't be taken seriously'

If a presenter is not known for being humorous then the sudden injection of humour into his text may well seem as incongruous as donning a Max Miller suit.

However, if he is not known to his audience then he should not assume that a judicious injection of relevant humour will undermine his serious intent.

There is a common misconception – that you can't be both amusing and serious. Why this should be when the world's leading communicators prove the exact opposite baffles me.

Of course it demands control. But you don't have to be a Shakespeare, Shaw, Wilde, Mark Twain or Voltaire to make your serious points lightheartedly.

Think like the listener you are the rest of the time. Or the student you were. As the Talmud teaches, 'Only the lesson which is enjoyed is learned well.'

You *can* be serious and amusing. Try not to be *earnest*. That is seriousness which take itself seriously (my definition). The ability to laugh at yourself, to make your serious point in an amusing way, helps you establish rapport with and maintain the interest of your audience.

But note that humour is not simply a sop, a pause in the middle of a serious text, a commercial break which affords relief. Nor is it the spoonful of sugar which helps the medicine go down or the coating on the pill.

If humour is an integral part of your message – and especially if it can help express *your* point – then you will be taken seriously.

'Humour is a distraction'

Fundamentally this is true. A joke is a collision. Two thoughts come together. Paths cross. You are treading one path, then suddenly you're pitched forward into another.

The essence of humour is incongruity. Can you afford to be incongruous?

Yes – provided the incongruity is relevant.

There may be just cause for the occasional quip or aside which merely brings relief – the equivalent of stretching one's legs. But the humour otherwise must be integrated and relevant.

This is not as difficult as it seems. Books of jokes, anecdotes and epigrams abound – all suitably indexed – which can illustrate your theme.[2]

So the incongruity in the joke serves to reinforce your message.

But humour works best when the incongruity itself is relevant.

Jokes are based on ambiguity. There are two meanings – or two levels of meaning. The simplest example is a pun. The acid test of a pun in communication (especially in advertising) is 'would you bother to convey the secondary meaning if it were to stand alone?' If so, then the pun is worth telling.

A good pun is more than a self-conscious display of verbal dexterity, it is a felicitous coupling of appropriate thoughts. John Donne watching his mistress unrobe beseeches her:

To teach thee I am naked first; why then
What needs thou more covering than a man?

Some people allege that humour is irrelevant. They are right – *irrelevant* humour is irrelevant.

Relevant humour can surprise, wake up, revive an audience; add a new dimension to something you have already said; make people see something in an entirely new way.

The essence of good humour is essence. It's distilled. The epigram, the one-liner, the quip and the best jokes . . . are sparse. Not a word is wasted. Humour can thus encapsulate much of your argument. It can become the conduit to the audience's mind for the two previous pages of text. A joke can do what Voltaire claims for poetry over prose – 'says more and in fewer words' (*Dictionnaire Philosophique*, 1764).

We saw earlier that a good joke teller is a good presenter. Because a joke is a perfect example of our communication model. A joke is two-way. It demands the participation of the respondent. The message has to be carefully coded. And the impact of the joke lies in the *decoding*. For this to work there has to be shared meaning between the transmitter and receiver. In fact *two* shared meanings. The overt one which is the code used for telling the story and the covert one which is used for blowing it up.

The appreciation of a second code involves a delayed response. This is the gap in the spark plug. The size of the gap affects the ignition. Too wide or too narrow – no spark.

The respondent has to respond. If not – no joke.

There is no joke without initial bewilderment. A microsecond of confusion followed by elucidation.

'Waiter, there's a fly in my soup.'
'Shall I bring another spoon?'

Mm? Ahh! The respondent has to *work it out*. Not a tough job but an activity all the same. And the presentation which encourages activity is more likely to be remembered.

If I tell an audience something it may listen. If I tell it a joke it not only listens, it takes part.

But what if the taking part is frustrated? If the audience doesn't get the joke? As we saw, it may mean I have misjudged the audience or mishandled the material. It is clearly the presenter's fault. But a communication fault – not a sin to be laid exclusively at the feet of humour. Remember, a joke which fails may be an indication of a failure in the presentation as a whole.

However, it is quite likely that the joke will not be appreciated by the entire audience. Funny bones may not be as personal as fingerprints but humour is subjective. There are degrees of subtlety in the material and degrees of familiarity in the audience. Do not be too disappointed if the entire house doesn't smile. If your address is aimed primarily at a certain section of the audience then the joke can help seek them out. An in-joke, a deeply coded message, may increase the rapport between you and those particular respondents. Although jokes may take place in public each initial act of communication is private. The in-joke flatters those who get it, establishes a bond between the transmitter and receiver and between the comprehending receivers. Too much of this may cause élitism and a disaffection among the rest of the audience.

It has to be used carefully.

Irony we've already warned against. It can trip up the most experienced presenter. Chambers defines it as the 'conveyance of meaning (generally satirical) by words whose literal meaning is the opposite'. You can be ironic in a small group of colleagues. They know you. So when you depart from your normal self, express opinions counter to the expected, they make the adjustment. In mixed company (i.e. with friends and strangers) irony may be a perfect way of communicating in code to your friends.

However, with a public audience, how can you say one thing and mean the opposite and simultaneously convey the fact that that's what you are doing? You can't say 'I am now going to be ironic', since that defeats the whole object. For it to work at all, irony has to be introduced once the audience has got to know you.

I once shared an audience with Bob Waterman, co-author of the US best seller *In Search of Excellence*, in a symposium on the British experience on the principles expounded in his book. I called my talk 'The other side of the water, man' and, in an assumed, pompous and disdainful upper-class voice, criticized the book for preaching nostrums totally inappropriate to the UK market.

Had I tried that among an audience of my friends and colleagues the penny would have dropped in half a minute. At this seminar before an audience of two hundred strangers I suffered twenty minutes of severe embarrassment. I was taken seriously. Worse still, many of the audience were clearly totally supportive of my alter ego. Getting back on track was difficult not only for me but for some of the audience.

I suffered a similar though briefer embarrassment when addresing a CBI seminar on the subject of speaking in public. I advised the audience to prepare their speech with the recipient in mind. 'Always imagine you're a listener in the audience.'

I paused and looked round the room.

'Now – will you please imagine you're a listener in the audience? Try very hard.'

I thought it was quite droll asking the listeners to imagine they were listeners. The listeners did not.

Another humorous trick to use with care is the aside. Used sparingly and well signalled (make the brackets audible) it can be very effective – if only as a moment's relief or evidence that you aren't as pompous as the previous phrase may have made you sound. The problem begins when the aside takes over, when there appear to be two speakers. Which is the real you – you or your dummy? Asides can so easily become criticisms – of the subject, the conference, other people, yourself.

But the most difficult problem for the novice is the maintenance of balance between the humorous and non-humorous parts of his presentation. Begin with a few jokes and the audience may not know when you have finished. It may puzzle over a joke which isn't. It may wait for a punchline which never comes. Conversely, the joke which follows a serious section may not be seen to be a joke.

But the problem is hugely reduced if you remember to think less about jokes and more about humour as a texture variant.

The more relevant and integrated the humour, the greater the chance of holding the audience. In the accomplished presentation it is not a matter of 'now serious, now funny', of comic relief. A presentation should resemble a slice of cassata. Sweeping swirls of theme integrated and highlighted with bits of nut and *glacé* fruit, the examples.

Great orators are able to vary the texture of their speeches, mixing emotions as a painter mixes colours on his palette. In the following extract from David Lloyd George's appeal to the nation in the second month of World War I, note how he uses both anger and mirth to win over the audience – virtually simultaneously.

It is the intent of Prussia to break the treaty, and she has done it. (*Hisses*) She avows it with cynical contempt for every principle of justice. She says 'Treaties only bind you when your interest is to keep them.' (*Laughter*) 'What is a treaty?', says the German Chancellor, 'A scrap of paper.' Have you any five pound notes about you? (*Laughter and applause*) I am not calling for them. (*Laughter*) Have you any of those neat little Treasury one pound notes? (*Laughter*) If you have, burn them; they are only scraps of paper (*Laughter and applause*) What are they made of? Rags. (*Laughter*) What are they worth? The whole credit of the British Empire. (*Loud applause*)

Questions to involve the audience. Irony – because *he* knows that *they* know. Humour integrated into the message and every bit as powerful and impassioned as the plain speaking. This is not hit-and-miss, now that now this. It is a thoroughly cohesive entity. The humour belongs by right as the gravedigger's jokes belong in *Hamlet*.

And note too how Lloyd George invites the listener to bridge the gap. The reference to five pound notes is oblique. Lloyd George does *not* say 'A five pound note is also a scrap of paper.' Instead he asks a question, 'Have you any five pound notes about you?' The *listener* makes the connection.

Humour is about participation.

So is presentation.

29 Rehearsals and Run-throughs

The purpose of rehearsal is to eliminate noise. Rehearsal begins as soon as your text is written. Your first reading aloud is rehearsal. It should tell you how easy your text is to speak and where the problems are. It should help you turn text into script. The markings will be a response to the trial and error of rehearsal – in your office or bedroom. Familiarize yourself with the script. Know the material, sight-read the pages, know where the visual aids appear. But reading the script silently to yourself is not enough. You must hear yourself (ideally with a tape recorder) and you must time yourself. Presentation is a time art like music, drama, ballet. Reading a score or a play script is not rehearsal.

But the real rehearsal, the subject of this and the following chapter – let's call it a *dress* rehearsal – occurs a day or two before the presentation, very often on the day itself. Unless the conference is rather special there will be only one rehearsal, though there should also be a meeting of speakers and organizers some weeks before the event at which the presenters will have been briefed and told about the equipment and the order of events, and will have become acquainted with each other and each other's arguments. Overlap and repetition will have been discussed. It is important to discover not only what issues your fellow speakers are addressing, but what examples and what aids they are using. You may decide to eliminate duplicated items. You may decide to use your material differently. You may decide to go ahead and repeat what another speaker is saying.

What matters is that you *know* – before the day. Nothing tells the audience that the conference is badly organized as much as duplicated material catching the presenter unawares. Furthermore it reveals that the second speaker was not in the audience during the first presentation or wasn't paying attention.

The dress rehearsal, then, should not find you unfamiliar with your material or that of your fellow speakers. Nor, with luck and good management, should you be unaware of the presentation room or, in the broadest sense, the equipment. After all, you will have informed the organizers of your needs and they will have informed you of their means of satisfying them.

Nevertheless, never assume!

I once specified a Sony U-Matic video tape player and a Kodak carousel slide projector and arrived (from a previous function) twenty minutes before a presentation to discover a VHS machine and a Leitz Pradovit. In neither case did the software fit the hardware.

In this instance I was unable to rehearse in anything approaching ideal conditions. Though these are very rarely attained.

Ideally the dress rehearsal should take place in exactly the same conditions in which the presentation itself will be made.

This means that the location must be the same. As must the equipment, the operators, the lighting, the set, the props and all the speaker-support material. And that the presentation has to be delivered, in full, in the time scheduled, with *all* the pauses, effects and allowances for audience reaction. All that seems obvious.

Less obvious are other factors which can create noise.

In my experience the main problem with dress rehearsals is that they take place in front of the wrong people at the wrong time of day.

Very few people in the audience are actually listening. They have other

*The main problem with dress
rehearsals is that they take
place in front of the wrong
people*

things to do. They are talking, almost certainly about their part in the
conference. Even the most experienced presenter gets miffed by this lack of
feedback and excess of literal noise. He responds by gabbling his speech
and the organizers, probably in a hurry, respond to him by suggesting that
rather than have a complete dress rehearsal they have a 'mechanical
run-through'.

What this entails is a thorough check of all the mechanical aids – the
lighting, the slide projector, the videotape machine, the flipchart, etc. – in
performance, i.e. how they are cued, and how and by whom operated.
Movements on and off the stage, at and away from the lectern, are
rehearsed.

A mechanical run-through is clearly essential. And if there is little time for
rehearsal it is more important to get that completely right than do a half
rehearsal at true delivery speed.

Nevertheless, it is far from satisfactory. Ideally there should be a full dress
rehearsal *plus* a mechanical run-through.

Ideally too there should be one or two people in the audience whose job
it is to listen, preferably people unacquainted with the text.

(If this were show-biz you wouldn't just have a dress rehearsal, you'd
have a preview.)

The other problem with dress rehearsals – the wrong time of day – is
often less apparent till it's too late, i.e. on the day itself.

If you're presenting at, say, 11 a.m., what happens usually at that time?

You can bet it's not what happens at your rehearsal time of 7.30 p.m. For one thing where is the sun? How about traffic noise? Could that possibly be the time the coffee lady comes in? Or the air conditioning comes on? Are they preparing lunch in the adjacent room? Where are the phones? (You hadn't thought of phones? Could that be because they are silent at 7.30 p.m.?)

The previous paragraph was written from the heart. I was asked to address the Greek Advertising Association at Cape Sounion, south of Athens. I arrived the evening before. The room was huge. There was a large screen at one end, a slide projector in the middle, in the aisles, and a 35 mm film projector at the back. I gave a marked copy of the script to the film projectionist and acquainted myself with the panel on the lectern. The lights were lowered. We began.

The rehearsal was perfect. All the cues worked. The images were pin sharp. The sound was right.

I went to bed almost happy.

At 9 a.m. I was back in the room ready for a 9.30 start. Something was bugging. The room was filled with that iridescent light of a Greek high summer. Outside – through the window behind the stage – the sky was uninterrupted blue.

I went up to the producer.

'Where are the curtains?'

He pointed to the white lacery adorning the windows.

'No – the black-out curtains.'

There were *no* black-out curtains. We had a quick trial run of slides and film. The daylight completely killed the image of the film. The light intensity

of the slide projector was a bit greater but the image was barely doing justice to the material.

I shrugged despairingly.

'Don't worry. We will fix it. You start and we will fix it.'

I started.

I showed slides. I ran a film or two. I explained the pictures.

Ten minutes into this non-event, banging began. I looked round. Behind me, behind the window, behind the screen, two hotel workers were noisily erecting a wooden fence. This had the effect of 'holding' the image. The audience could now see the films but not hear them. . .

But the dress rehearsal had gone well. In fact too well. Actors are generally worried when that happens, when they've nothing to worry about.

The purpose of a dress rehearsal is to discover problems. Before it's too late. If you get a cue wrong, stumble over a line, screen an upside-down slide and in embarrassment apologize, the producer is bound to say something like 'That's why we have rehearsals.'

It'll be all right on the night precisely because the dress rehearsal has detected the latent noise.

30 The Dress Rehearsal

At a conference the time set aside for rehearsals is rarely filled. You will notice, however, that the presenters who take their full allotment are precisely those whose professionalism leads you to believe they don't need to rehearse at all.

To repeat, ideally you should

Rehearse in exactly the same conditions in which the presentation will be made.

Of course, by definition, this can't happen. The audience, if you get one, won't be the same. The time might be the same but the day certainly can't be. The atmosphere won't be.

Nevertheless, unless you aim for the ideal your sights might be too low.

You will need first to know who's who. Who is in charge? Who will be helping you? Who will be introducing you?

And – silly, you may think, but in fact crucial – will the people at the rehearsal be there on the day? Is the projectionist you're briefing the one who will actually press the button? Come to that, will the equipment be the same?

You will need a checklist. The purpose of this – as with any checklist – is to guard against accidental exclusion. Exclude nothing.

Rehearse everything. **Everything**.

Environment, equipment, support system – interaction

Dress

It's called a dress rehearsal. Wear the clothes you intend wearing. You will feel more comfortable in them on the day. If you intend wearing a jacket and tie or a suit, and rehearse in a blouson and open-necked shirt or blouse, not only the effect on the audience will be different but *you* will be different. (Or are you the exception – the person indifferent to the clothes he puts on?) What's more, unless you rehearse in the same clothes you may be thrown by the equipment and ancillary items which come into contact with your person. If it's a radio mike where will they put the small but heavy box (the transmitter)? If it's a throat mike to what do they clip it? If you are going to demonstrate by taking something out of your pocket – which pocket? Will you be wearing a conference badge? Will that catch the light – on your lapel but not when it's on your top pocket? Will your pocket handkerchief or your scarf be in the way? What other noise are you generating?

For example, will you wear spectacles? Will you remove them? Why? When?

Lectern

Is it the right height? Where are the buttons? Does it incorporate a clock? Is it angled correctly for the screen and the audience? Does it accommodate the script – in two piles, remember, which move right to left? Does it have a reading light? Does the reading light interfere with the screen? Can you switch it off and on? Can you read your script? Are all the colours of your colour code visible – especially the red? Is there storage space for any props?

Slide operation

Is there a remote control system? Is it part of the lectern or separate? Is it attached to a cord, or radio controlled? Do you have to point the controller at the projector? Where is the projector? If you're not controlling the slides then make sure you give the projectionist a marked script. How quickly do the slides respond to the button? Are your cue marks accurate?

Slide projector

Do your slides work in the location and at the agreed lighting level? Are they all hitting, filling, the screen? If there are any dodgy slides remove them and replace with blanks. Of course these should have been checked well in advance but it's better to remove them now than apologize tomorrow. Check for yourself how your slides look from the back of the room. Have you allowed for enough blanks – especially when switching to other equipment?

Will your slides be projected on the day exactly as at the rehearsal? For example, is it front or back projection, i.e. in front of or behind the screen?

Front projected slides are loaded in the carousel upside down and back to front. Back projected slides are loaded upside down and right way round.

Front projection may mean the projection is in the room itself. If so, where? Does it obstruct the view for some of the audience? Will the noise of the fan affect reception?

Video playback machine

Familiarize yourself with the equipment if you are due to operate it. If not, make sure the operator has a marked script. Check how long is necessary for run-up. Have you allowed sufficient time (and provided sufficient leader) between each segment of tape? Is the image on the screen well defined? How about the monitors – are there enough and are they in the right places? Sit in different chairs around the room and check.

Overhead projector

Does the image hit, fill, the screen? Is it accessible? Which way round do you put the acetates? Is there a convenient place for *two* sets of acetates – used and unused? Are there acetate pens (plenty of them)? Is there a card big enough to hide the entire image and can it slide easily along the acetate to reveal items? Where's the switch?

Sound system

Ask somebody to speak your script and then check. Can you hear in all parts of the room? Is there mechanical feedback (e.g. if the event is being recorded are the two sound systems interacting?). What happens when the volume is raised, when the films or tapes are screened? Are the speakers balanced? If two presenters are performing is there a contrast of levels? Is there echo? Is there a hotel sound system and is it likely to interfere with the conference system?

Microphone

If you're using a stand-up mike, are you happy with its height? Are you sufficiently near without popping your Ps? Can you still see the audience? If it's a neck mike is there a danger of your accidentally banging it? Remember you're *live* and, if you're wired up, don't walk too far from your original position. If you have to put on your neck or clip mike yourself – rehearse it. If someone else – make sure you know who it is.

Lighting

Check the black-out (remember Greece!). Check the lighting levels for each part of your presentation. Will it have to change for the showing of slides, film, OHP? Try not to arrange too many changes of level. These irritate the audience. Occasional changes, on the other hand, provide drama and relief.

Be careful, especially if there is no lectern light or there is no light switch on the lectern, that you don't lose your script when the lights change. The lectern light might in fact be a spot above your head, which goes out when the screen is in use.

Again, see how it looks from the middle and back of the room. And check where the light switches are.

Sight lines

Can you be seen by everyone? Can you see everyone? Can the screen be seen? Does one piece of equipment get in the way of the screen? Do *you* get in the way?

The set

What is it saying about the presentation – before it begins? (See Chapter 22.) Is it contributing noise, e.g. asking questions, making suggestions about what will follow? Are the chairs at the table, stage right, there for a purpose – or are they left over from a previous presentation?

Movements

Rehearse *all* your movements. Where will you be just prior to your presentation? What's your cue for moving? How do you get to your speaking position? How long does that take? How do you cover the pause? Will the first the audience sees of you be your back? Can you improve the move? For example, could you, by the use of lighting, be discovered at the lectern?

Familiarize yourself with the stage area. How many steps does it take to move to the overhead projector? How far will the neck mike cord allow you to come from the lectern?

How do you end? Where will you be? If you answer questions, where from? How do you leave the stage? And what do you leave behind? What is *that* saying about you?

The room

Similarly you should familiarize yourself with the complete environment. Ideally of course you should know it already. Enlist others' opinions about heating and ventilation. Check literal noise. Look for areas of potential problems – e.g. doors, windows.

Props

Do you have a pointer? If a laser pointer is provided make sure you practise. The small red arrow is useful for pointing out key features but irritating if it wanders all over the screen – and unsettling if it indicates the shaking hand of a nervous speaker!

Will you need water? Where is the glass, the carafe? Is it plain water?

Decline fizzy. It may make you pause in mid-sentence not for effect but relief. (Perrier is noisy.)

Your performance

So far we have been discussing the environment, equipment and support system and your interaction with them. Now we discuss you, your performance.

You must *rehearse in full*. It must take the time you have allotted according to the formula on p. 62. You must give the rehearsal your best shot. Do not withhold anything for the day itself. The extra boost in performance on the day comes not from withholding the night before but from the increase in adrenaline provided by the occasion itself and the interaction with the audience.

Unless you rehearse in full – with every gesture, every movement, using all your visual aids, running your films in their entirety – you will not appreciate the total effect of your presentation. Rehearse and you may eliminate unwanted surprises.

You must *rehearse at the correct speed*. This includes pauses. You must make allowances for audience participation. Unless you do this the timing will be meaningless.

You must *practise looking at the four corners* of the room. Not easy with nobody there – but essential. Believe me, looking at the room makes you less nervous. So does sitting in a lot of the seats.

You must *practise all your gestures*. By now most of these should be second nature. However, you may be gesturing unknowingly and communicating signals against your text. You may be fidgeting with your spectacles. Ask a colleague to comment frankly on this aspect of your performance. You may have to cut your gestures down, spend more time holding the sides of the lectern.

You must *practise light and shade*. Your script should be marked for variations in pace, volume, pitch.

You must *practise your introduction*. This includes your thanks. And your *conclusion*. This includes your handover. Sloppiness can mar the most important parts of your presentation – the beginning and ending.

You're in charge. That may not be absolutely true but the audience believes you are. You should certainly be in charge of your material. And you can't let the equipment dictate, can you?

That, I'm afraid, is easier said than done. We have seen that the shape of the room, the arrangement of the chairs, the look of the set can all transmit signals. We have met Veltrusky's dictum, 'all that is on the stage is a sign'.

The wrong equipment – i.e. equipment you are not expecting or had not commissioned or had not familiarized yourself with – may not merely diminish your performance, it may actually change its nature.

The simplest example is the absence of a microphone. The room may not need it – although you may because, for example, you wish to talk intimately. Those intimate friendly phrases change character when declaimed.

The complex truth of this fact concerning the potency of the equipment was brought home to me recently when I was asked to give an after-dinner talk to about fifty guests at a client meeting in a hotel ballroom.

There was, alas, no time for rehearsal. I had anticipated using a stand-up or neck mike and a table lectern. It was a so-called conference hotel.

Never assume.

Half-way through the main course I discovered there was a hand-held mike with a trailing cord – and no lectern.

Luckily I had prepared cards rather than a sheaf of papers. So I could just hold the mike in one hand and the cards in the other.

However, the absence of a lectern and the presence of a trailing mike meant that I could not gesture. Both hands were occupied. More significantly, the set-up meant that the moment I stood up I was no longer the after-dinner speaker, I was the *cabaret*.

The host introduced me on the floor. He handed me the trailing mike. I could not then move back to the table. Though I could move anywhere else. Not to move was a negation of the equipment.

From the table with a table lectern I could be semi-serious. The jokes would illustrate my theme. From the floor with a hand-held mike the jokes were the *raison d'être*.

I had become a comedian. It wasn't exactly a disaster. But if only I had been able to rehearse...

Rehearsal helps you take charge – because it enables you to eliminate unwanted surprises. But first, of course, you need to anticipate them.

Ask yourself – what's the worst that could happen?

The projector has jammed...

My mike's packed up...

Im miles behind the clock...

I've lost my place...

The power has failed

Smile, damn you, SMILE!

- *The projection bulb blows.* Is there a spare? How long will it take to replace? Can you dispense with some slides?
- *The projector jams.* How disastrous is the presentation without any slides? Which visual aids would you have to describe? How would you do this?
- *The sound system packs up.* How good are the acoustics for the unaided voice? How much of the presentation would be carried by the visual aids?
- *You lose your place.* How soon can you find it again? This is easy to practise. It is a good test of the marking of your speech.
- *You fall behind the clock* – despite all your rehearsals. What do you cut? Is it marked in the script?
- *The power goes.* How good are you at jokes by candlelight?

If you can keep your head while all about you ... then you're in charge, my son.

31 The Day

The day of the conference has arrived. It seems an age since you began collecting your thoughts. You then arranged them into an argument. You had your theme. You defined the *point* of your presentation. You structured it, made it make sense to a listener, taking him step by step through time by ordering the sentences; and to the future audience by planning your visual aids. You timed it, revised it. You turned your text into a script. You discussed your approach with others – on and off the platform. You rehearsed privately and publicly. In a few hours you will present.

Stay loose.

Remain flexible. There is still work to be done on the presentation – apart from the delivery itself. The script you've written is unlikely to be the exact script you speak.

Do not get locked into your manuscript.

Have a final rehearsal in your room. Full, out loud, allowing for visuals and pauses and audience participation.

Check the timing. If necessary make final cuts. Nobody will blame you for underrunning.

But remember a rehearsal is not the show. Yesterday's dress rehearsal is not the show. Only the show is the show. The script in your hand will be departed from.

Read the morning paper. Listen to the news. Has anything happened to affect your presentation? Has an important fact or statistic changed? Is your argument attacked or reinforced by a news item? Or, more likely, is there a news item which you could introduce lightheartedly, *en passant*, to establish rapport with the audience? Topicality scores high marks. By definition the audience could not have heard the remark before. It proves to them that this exact presentation has never been given previously. And it demonstrates that the presenter is in charge – and flexible.

Flexibility is key. Do not become an automaton. One of the disadvantages of a good dress rehearsal is the wish to repeat it on the day. The presentation is not a repeat – it's *live*.

Get some fresh air. You may be spending all day in artificial air.

Arrive at the location early. Get to know the room before the delegates come in. Check everything is where you expect it to be. Have any changes been made? You may still be able to do something about any problems this causes.

Spend a little time with the crew. They will be busy but if you are efficient and thorough you will win their respect and earn their time. Hand over your slides, tapes, etc. and cued script (if you haven't done so the day before). Make sure everything is clearly marked with your name. If there are several speakers at this conference also indicate the time of your presentation.

If you hand in a carousel of slides mark your name on the bottom as well as the transparent plastic top. (Tops can be transferred!)

Check the equipment.

Have a mechanical run-through. This will reassure you that all the slides are hitting and filling the screen with the correct image. But make sure you check them against your script. Run through your other visual aids.

Carry a first-aid kit. The contents will depend upon the occasion and the complexity of the equipment, but an all-purpose kit might consist of blank slides, acetate pen, elastic bands, post-it notes, spare bulb, penknife, Durabeam torch, aspirins, indigestion tablets, throat lozenges – and a complete, marked-up spare copy of the script.

Soon the audience will begin to arrive. Ask for a delegates list. Analyse it. How does the audience break down in terms of sex, company type, level of seniority, geographical location? Any foreigners? Can you introduce a fact or two about *this* audience into your speech, preferably something relevant to your theme?

Mingle with them over the welcome cup of coffee. Don't stay too long with one person. You have every reason to excuse yourself. Get to know them. The audience is half of the dialogue.

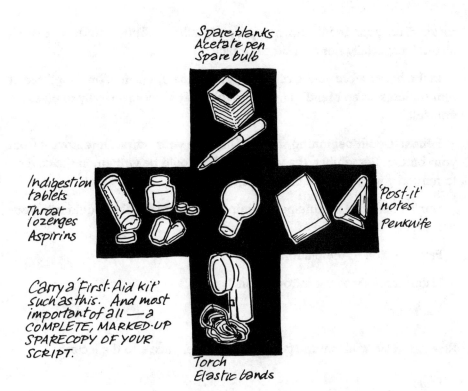

Spare blanks
Acetate pen
Spare bulb

Indigestion
tablets
Throat
lozenges
Aspirins

'Post-it'
notes
Penknife

Carry a 'First-Aid kit'
such as this. And most
important of all — a
COMPLETE, MARKED-UP
SPARECOPY OF YOUR
SCRIPT.

Torch
Elastic bands

What have they come for? What do they expect to get out of it? Sense the atmosphere – indifference, expectancy, excitement? Keep an ear open for noise.

Get into the room five minutes before the conference starts. Watch how the room fills up. Is there a revealing emptiness at the front? Where are the people you were speaking to?

Attend everything that precedes your presentation. It may give you material. It will teach you about the audience. It will alert you to any problems – and opportunities.

Listen carefully to the introduction to the conference. It sets the context. You may wish to refer to it.

Listen and watch the sessions. Make notes.

If you're speaking after lunch, use the break more for feedback than feeding. Assess the audience's reaction to the morning. Do not eat much. As Dunckel and Parnham advise in *The Business Guide to Effective Speaking*, 'no matter what time of the day you speak you want your blood focused on your brain and not your digestion'.[1] Above all do not drink alcohol. Especially not for Dutch courage.

In the hour before you're on try to get into the open air, if only for three or four minutes' deep breathing. And go to the washroom – if only to reassure yourself.

Rehearse your beginning silently. Unstaple your script. Or remove it from your binder. Remember, the word 'CODE' should be written on the cover – to remind you to think of the audience.

Don't suck a last minute peppermint. Bits on your palate could ruin your delivery.

Pay attention to the platform.

Listen carefully to the introduction.

You're on!

Rise naturally, walk naturally – at your normal pace – to the lectern.

Smile.

It relaxes the audience. It may even relax you. A blank look says nothing. A frown is a disconcerting message. A smile establishes *contact.*

Pause.

Very briefly look at the audience ... all parts of it ... and begin.

Respond to the introduction . Make it relevant and personal rather than an all-purpose curt acknowledgement. A natural thank you to another human being.

This means ad-libbing, looking at the chairperson and the audience – and *not at your script.*

You are establishing contact. You may get audience feedback – laughter, applause even. Do not go on too long. Start your presentation.

But keep your eyes away from your script.

You *know* the beginning by heart. Go for it. Paraphrase if necessary. Don't rush. You can afford to take your time. The audience is sizing you up. And you're doing the same. Maintain the contact. Look down when you have to. And make sure you deliver the cues exactly as scripted – for the projectionist or yourself.

If you've put the presentation together then it should not be too difficult to put it across.

Don't *read* the script. Refer to it. Remind yourself of the next line or two and then deliver them to the audience.

Your marked script has become a set of notes.

Remember you were *given* the audience's attention. Now you must gain and maintain their *interest*.

Be enthusiastic.

Attack. Project.

You believe in what you say – otherwise why say it? Convey that belief.

Look at the audience. Go round the room. Never look away at the end of a sentence – but after it.

Keep an eye on the clock (if your lectern doesn't have one, put your watch in front of you) and the page numbers.

Don't forget your markings. Change pace, pitch, volume where you need to. Don't forget to pause, to gesture ...

Before you know it, you're beginning to enjoy it. It's not quite what you imagined. It's *like* the rehearsal but different somehow. That charge wasn't there yesterday.

This is ... *live*.

It went well. You felt in charge. The chairperson then says, 'Are there are any questions?' If there are, the audience may soon be in charge. If you've prepared a good argument then the questions may be few. If nobody raises a question this could indicate acceptance of your argument or, possibly, a total rejection. Either way the audience's mind is made up.

Try to avoid questions in public. Offer to answer them informally.

But the decision is rarely yours to make and you must be prepared for questions.

Make sure that the question is clearly understood. It may mean repeating the question, even questioning or interrupting the questioner to establish the main point he is making. Do not let questioners make speeches. Relate the question to your presentation. Make your answer equally clear, short and to the point. *Your* point.

Do not be tempted to comment on something outside your presentation topic.

Some questioners are critical because you did not make the presentation they would have made. They are out of court. Try to remain in charge. After all, the subject of this question period is your presentation.

Use the question period to reinforce your argument.

Support your answers if necessary by direct reference to your script.

And always keep something in reserve for question time. This does not mean withholding a key element of your speech against the possibility of being asked an appropriate question. It does mean, however, having spare examples, illustrations, anecdotes which echo an argument or, better still, play to your main point. Maybe one or two of the 'desirable' pieces you reluctantly cut when timing your speech (Chapter 17). I also, if possible, add a few slides after the final blanks and a duplicate slide of the main point or a summary.

Don't be afraid of repeating yourself. And above all – on the final question – make the answer lead inevitably to *your* conclusion. The thought you want to leave with the audience.

Handled properly, question time can underline your authority. If the presentation is the tip of the iceberg your answers can prove there *is* an iceberg beneath the surface.

It's almost over. Thank the audience. Thank the chairman. And thank the crew.

How did it go? You'll know soon enough. Don't ask that question direct. (People are generally too kind.) Answer other people's questions. Stay around as long as you can and listen to comments. And ask subsidiary questions. Could they hear when you went off-mike? Were the slides on long enough? Too long? Did they understand the point of a particular slide? Were they convinced by a certain statistic? Did they think you overstated this, underplayed that? Were they surprised by the ending – how it came out? Did they get the point? But above all ... *Did you achieve your target response?*

If you don't know, ask Eric.

Notes

Chapter 1   Structure and Execution

1   Cicero, *De Oratore Books I–II*, tr. E.W. Sutton and H. Rackham, Loeb Classical Library (Harvard University Press, Cambridge, Mass., and William Heinemann, London, 1942).

2   Plato, *Phaedrus and Letters VII and VIII*, tr. Walter Hamilton, Penguin Classics (Penguin Books, Harmondsworth, 1973).

Chapter 2   Write the Speech

1   Cicero, *De Oratore Books I–II*, tr. E.W. Sutton and H. Rackham, Loeb Classical Library (Harvard University Press, Cambridge, Mass., and William Heinemann, London, 1942).

2   Walter J. Ong, *Orality and Literacy, The Technologizing of the Word*, New Accents, general ed. Terence Hawkes (Methuen, London, 1982).

3   Barry T. Turner, *Effective Technical Writing and Speaking* (Business Books, London, 1974).

4   William Strunk Jr, *The Elements of Style*, revised E.B. White, 3rd edn (Macmillan Publishing, New York, 1973).

5   Turner, *Effective Technical Writing and Speaking*.

6   *Teaching of English*, quoted in Sir Ernest Gowers, *The Complete Plain Words*, 2nd edn (Penguin Books, Harmondsworth, 1973).

7   Ong, *Orality and Literacy*.

8   Quoted in Robert Graves and Alan Hodge, *The Reader over your Shoulder: Handbook for Writers of English Prose* (Jonathan Cape, London, 1943).

9   Ong, *Orality and Literacy*.

10   Cicero, *De Oratore*.

11   Cicero, *De Oratore*.

12   Cicero, *De Oratore*.

13   Cicero, *De Oratore*.

14   Longinus, *On the Sublime*, tr. T.S. Dorsch, Penguin Classics (Penguin Books, Harmondsworth, 1965).

Chapter 3   Basic Communication

1   Based upon the model of C. Shannon and W. Weaver, *The Mathematical Theory of Communication* (University of Illinois, 1982).

2   Entry on rhetoric in *Encyclopaedia Britannica*, 15th edn (Helen Hemingway Benton, Chicago, 1974).

3   Walter J. Ong, *Orality and Literacy*,

The Technologizing of the Word, New Accents, general ed. Terence Hawkes (Methuen, London, 1982).

4 Terence Hawkes, *Structuralism and Semiotics* (Methuen, London, 1977).

Chapter 4 Think Like a Listener

1 Antony Jay, *Effective Presentation: The Communication of Ideas by Words and Visual Aids* (British Institute of Management, London, 1971).

2 Jay, *Effective Presentation*.

3 Robert Graves and Alan Hodge, *The Reader over your Shoulder: Handbook for Writers of English Prose* (Jonathan Cape, London, 1943).

4 Jay, *Effective Presentation*.

5 Cicero, *De Oratore Books I–II*, tr. E.W. Sutton and H. Rackham, Loeb Classical Library (Harvard University Press, Cambridge, Mass., and William Heinemann, London, 1942).

6 Walter J. Ong, *Orality and Literacy, The Technologizing of the Word*, New Accents, general ed. Terence Hawkes (Methuen, London, 1982).

Chapter 5 Purpose and Point

1 David Bernstein, *Creative Advertising* (Longman, London, 1974).

2 William Goldman, *Adventures in the Screen Trade* (Macdonald, London, 1984).

3 Entry on rhetoric in *Encyclopaedia Britannica*, 15th edn (Helen Hemingway Benton, Chicago, 1974).

Chapter 6 Assembly

1 T.S. Eliot, 'The Metaphysical Poets', in *Selected Essays* (Faber & Faber, London, 1951).

2 C.E. Montague, *A Writer's Notes on his Trade* (Chatto & Windus, London, 1930).

3 Montague, *A Writer's Notes*.

Chapter 7 Patterns of Presentation

1 Cicero, *De Oratore Books I–II*, tr. E.W. Sutton and H. Rackham, Loeb Classical Library (Harvard University Press, Cambridge, Mass., and William Heinemann, London, 1942).

2 S.T. Coleridge, *Shakespearian Criticism*, ed. T.M. Raysor, Cambridge, Mass., 1930).

3 M. Cohen and E. Nagel, *An Introduction to Logic*, quoted in H.A. Shearring and B.C. Christian, *Reports – and How to Write Them* (George Allen & Unwin, London, 1965).

4 Plato, *Phaedrus and Letters VII and VIII*, tr. Walter Hamilton, Penguin Classics (Penguin Books, Harmondsworth, 1973).

Chapter 8 Beginnings

1 Quintilian, *Institutio Oratoria*, Outline of Great Books (Amalgamated Press, London).

Chapter 9 Middles

1 Antony Jay, *Effective Presentation: The Communication of Ideas by Words and Visual Aids* (British Institute of Management, London, 1971).

Chapter 10   Endings

1 Quintilian, *Institutio Oratoria*, Outline of Great Books (Amalgamated Press, London).

2 Quintilian, *Institutio Oratoria*.

3 Leo Burnett, *Communications of an Advertising Man* (private publication).

Chapter 11   Structuring the Language

1 George Orwell, 'Politics and the English Language', in *Shooting an Elephant and Other Essays* (A.M. Heath & Co, London, 1945).

Chapter 12   The Language of Speech

1 Walter J. Ong, *Orality and Literacy, The Technologizing of the Word*, New Accents, general ed. Terence Hawkes (Methuen, London, 1982).

2 Munro E. Edmonson, *Lore: An Introduction to the Science of Folklore and Literature*, quoted in Ong, *Orality and Literacy*.

3 Ong, *Orality and Literacy*.

4 Ong. *Orality and Literacy*.

Chapter 13   The Language Toolkit

1 Simeon Potter, *Our Language* (Penguin Books, Harmondsworth, 1950).

2 Potter, *Our Language*.

3 I am indebted to Simeon Potter for the classification of sentences.

4 Potter, *Our Language*.

5 Robert Graves and Alan Hodge, *The Reader over your Shoulder: Handbook for Writers of English Prose* (Jonathan Cape, London, 1943).

6 John Fairfax and John Moat, *The Way to Write* (Elm Tree Books, London, 1981).

7 Ernest Fenollosa, *The Chinese Written Character as a Medium for Poetry*, quoted in C. Butler and A. Fowler, *Topics in Criticism* (Longman, London, 1971).

8 Longinus, *On the Sublime*, tr. T.S. Dorsch, Penguin Classics (Penguin Books, Harmondsworth, 1965).

9 T.S. Eliot, 'Preludes', in *The Complete Plays and Poems* (Faber & Faber, London, 1969).

Chapter 14   Imagery

1 Sir Herbert Read, *English Prose Style* (G. Bell & Sons, London, 1952).

Chapter 15   Style

1 Quoted in John Fairfax and John Moat, *The Way to Write* (Elm Tree Books, London, 1981).

2 Quintilian, *Institutio Oratoria*, Outline of Great Books (Amalgamated Press, London).

3 Michael du Cann, *The Art of the Advocate* (Penguin Books, Harmondsworth, 1964).

4 George Orwell, 'Politics and the English Language', in *Shooting an Elephant and Other Essays* (A.M. Heath & Co, London, 1945).

Chapter 16   Noise

1 J. Lyons, *Non Verbal Communi-*

cation, ed. R.A. Hinde (Cambridge University Press, Cambridge, 1972).

2   Robert Graves and Alan Hodge, *The Reader over your Shoulder: Handbook for Writers of English Prose* (Jonathan Cape, London, 1943).

Chapter 17   Text into Script

1   John May, *How to Make Effective Business Presentations – and Win!* (McGraw-Hill (UK), Maidenhead, 1983).

2   Quintilian, *Institutio Oratoria*.

Chapter 19   Visual Aids – The Slide

1   John May, *How to Make Effective Business Presentations – and Win!* (McGraw-Hill (UK), Maidenhead, 1983).

Chapter 20   Visual Aids – The Other Aids

1   John May, *How to Make Effective Business Presentations – and Win!* (McGraw-Hill (UK), Maidenhead, 1983).

2   May, *Effective Business Presentations*.

Chapter 22   The Room

1   Antony Jay, *Effective Presentation: The Communication of Ideas by Words and Visual Aids* (British Institute of Management, London, 1971).

Chapter 23   Delivery

1   Quintilian, *Institutio Oratoria*, Outline of Great Books (Amalgamated Press, London).

2   Quintilian, *Institutio Oratoria*.

3   Terence Hawkes, *Structuralism and Semiotics* (Methuen, London, 1977).

4   Quintilian, *Institutio Oratoria*.

5   Christopher Turk, *Effective Speaking: Communicating in Speech* (E. & F.N. Spon, London, 1985).

Chapter 24   In Control of Yourself

1   Quintilian, *Institutio Oratoria*, Outline of Great Books (Amalgamated Press, London).

2   Jacqueline Dunckel and Elizabeth Parnham, *The Business Guide to Effective Speaking* (Kogan Page, London, 1985).

3   Quoted in J. Lyons, *Non Verbal Communication*, ed. R.A. Hinde (Cambridge University Press, Cambridge, 1972).

4   Quoted in Lyons, *Non Verbal Communication*.

5   Quoted in Lyons, *Non Verbal Communication*.

6   John May, *How to Make Effective Business Presentations – and Win!* (McGraw-Hill (UK), Maidenhead, 1983).

Chapter 25   Holding the Audience

1   A. L. Kirkpatrick, *The Complete Speaker's Manual* (Thorsons, Wellingborough, 1983).

Chapter 26   Presenter and Equipment

1   Keir Elam, *The Semiotics of Theatre and Drama*, New Accents, general ed. Terence Hawkes (Methuen, London, 1980).

2   Elam, *Semiotics*.

3 Elam, *Semiotics.*

4 Elam, *Semiotics.*

5 Elam, *Semiotics.*

6 Quoted in Elam, *Semiotics.*

7 Elam, *Semiotics.*

Chapter 27   Drama

1 John Whiting, *The Art of the Dramatist and Other Pieces* (Alan Ross: London Magazine Editions, London, 1969).

2 Whiting, *Art of the Dramatist.*

3 Entry on drama in *Encyclopaedia Britannica*, 15th edn (Helen Hemingway Benton, Chicago, 1974).

Chapter 28   Humour

1 David Bernstein, *Creative Advertising* (Longman, London, 1974).

2 Edmund Fuller (ed.), *2500 Anecdotes for All Occasions* (Avenel Books, New York, 1978).

3 Herbert V. Prochnow and Herbert V. Prochnow Jr, *The Public Speaker's Treasure Chest* (Harper & Row, New York, 1977).

4 James Sutherland (ed.), *Oxford Book of Literary Anecdotes* (Oxford University Press, 1975).

Chapter 31   The Day

1 Jacqueline Dunckell and Elizabeth Parnham, *The Business Guide to Effective Speaking* (Kogan Page, London, 1985).

Index

Abbott, David 183
abstract words 82, 126
accent 23
accidents, textual *see* noise
acronyms 48
action
   in dramatic unities 51, 179–80
   by presenter 158–61, 205
   sharing in 28, 31, 64–5
active verbs 83–4
additive nature of speech 70, 75
adjectives 85–6
ad-libbing 11–12
adverbs 86
advertisements 36–7, 139–40
allegory 87
allusion 87
ambiguity 70, 91, 191
amplification 117, 118, 137, 138–9
anagnorisis 182
anarchic structure 50
anticlimax 93
antithesis 79, 93
anxiety *see* nerves
apostrophe 93–4
appearance 23, 161–2
Aristotle 173, 180
   on drama 51, 182
   on orators 26, 32, 34, 36
arrangement in rhetoric 149
asides 60, 194
assembly of material 38–42
association, unfortunate 99–100
attention *see under* audience
audience 8, 9, 23
   attention/attention curve 9, 31–2, 54–5, 58–9, 61, 152, 164
   feedback 21–2, 54, 168–71
   holding 164–71
   hostile and negative 29–30
   personality/composition of 29–30, 210
   researching 23
   target 18, 64, 89
   thinking like 26–33

   see also delivery; dialogue; drama; noise; receiver; room; sharing; visual aids
audio aids *see under* visual aids
augmentation 117, 118, 137, 138
autocue 133–4

'backloop', absence of 74
balanced sentence style 81
beginnings of presentation 32, 53–7
   see also introduction
blackboard 127
blank slides 120, 121, 122, 177
blood sugar, low 23
boards 117, 127, 128–9
body language *see* non-verbal
Buffon, Georges-Louis de 90
Burke, Edmund 94
Burnett, Leo 67

cards 113, 147
catalyst, working title as 41–2
categories 49
Cather, Willa 88
causation relationship 80, 102
channel noise 22, 165–6
character and situation in drama 180–1
Cheltenham Bold type 125
Churchill, Winston 76, 142
Cicero 16, 32–3
   on orators 9–10, 13, 43
circle, seating in 144
circumlocution 97
'class barrier' of language 73
classical structure 47
classification, standard 49
clichés 71–2, 88
climax 92, 153, 179, 181
clothes *see* dress
code
   language as 20–5, 96, 153
   noise 23, 165
co-existence relationship 80, 102
Coleridge, S.T. 45
collisions 39, 191

221